# Instrument
## Oral Exam Guide

by Michael D. Hayes

**Seventh Edition**

The comprehensive
guide to prepare you
for the FAA Oral Exam

**Aviation Supplies & Academics, Inc.**
Newcastle, Washington

*Instrument Oral Exam Guide*
*Seventh Edition*
by Michael D. Hayes

Aviation Supplies & Academics, Inc.
7005 132nd Place SE • Newcastle, Washington 98059-3153

Visit the ASA website often (**www.asa2fly.com**, Product Updates link or search "OEG-I7") to find updates posted there due to FAA regulation revisions that may affect this book. See also **www.asa2fly.com/reader/oegi** for the "Reader Resources" page with extra source material to download.

Printed in the United States of America

2013   2012                    9   8   7   6   5   4

**ASA-OEG-I7**
ISBN   1-56027-757-2
         978-1-56027-757-6

*Library of Congress Cataloging-in-Publication Data:*

Hayes, Michael D.
    Instrument oral exam guide : the comprehensive guide to prepare you for the FAA oral exam / by Michael D. Hayes. — [New ed.]
        p.    cm.
    "ASA-OEG-I" — Cover.
    Includes bibliographical references.
    1. Instrument flying — Examinations, questions, etc.   2. Aeronautics — Examinations, questions, etc.   3. United States. Federal Aviation Administration — Examinations, questions, etc. — Study guides.  I. Title.
TL711.B6H39  1996                              96-16988
629.132'5214'076—dc20                              CIP

*This guide is dedicated to the many talented students, pilots and flight instructors I have had the opportunity to work with over the years. Also, special thanks to Mark Hayes, Robert Hess, Meredyth Malocsay, and many others who supplied the patience, encouragement, and understanding necessary to complete the project.*

*— M.D.H.*

# Contents

## 3 En Route

## 4 Arrival

# Introduction

The *Instrument Oral Exam Guide* is a comprehensive guide designed for private or commercial pilots who are involved in training for the instrument rating. This guide was originally designed for use in a Part 141 flight school, but quickly became popular with those training under 14 CFR Part 61 not affiliated with an approved school. This book is also helpful for instrument-rated pilots who wish to refresh their knowledge or are preparing for an instrument proficiency check.

The guide is divided into four main sections which represent logical divisions of a typical instrument flight. An FAA examiner may ask questions from any of the subject areas within these divisions, at any time during the practical test, to determine if the applicant has the required knowledge. Through intensive post-instrument-checkride debriefings, we have provided you with the most consistent questions asked along with the information necessary for a knowledgeable response.

One area often overlooked in the FAA practical test standards is the "Introduction" section, yet it contains very important information concerning the practical test. There are two specific subjects discussed within the PTS Introduction that deserve closer attention: "Special Emphasis Areas" and "Single-Pilot Resource Management." Special emphasis areas are aircraft operations that are considered critical to flight safety — the result of statistical analysis of accident investigation findings and pilot operational errors. The examiner will also evaluate the applicant's ability throughout the practical test to use good single-pilot resource management (SRM), which is comprised of six basic tenets: aeronautical decision making, risk management, task management, situational awareness, CFIT awareness, and automation management. Although these areas may not be specifically addressed under each task, they are essential to flight safety and will be critically evaluated during the practical test. Additional study material pertaining to these areas are provided by links on an ASA "Reader Resource" webpage designed specifically for this Oral Exam Guide; these documents are available for download at the following address: **www.asa2fly.com/reader/oegi**.

*Continued*

At the end of this guide are three appendices. Appendix 1 has two checklists: the "Applicant's Practical Test Checklist," and the "Examiner's Practical Test Checklist" to be used when making final preparations for the instrument checkride. Appendix 2 contains the "Certified Flight Instructor—Instrument Airplane Supplement." This section provides additional study material for the CFII candidates preparing for the add-on to their existing CFI ticket. It also has study material of potential interest to all pilots preparing for the instrument checkride or an instrument proficiency check. Appendix 3 is an excerpt of the FAA's "Instrument Proficiency Check Guidance" document, a guide that assists a CFII in determining whether a pilot seeking an IPC endorsement has both the knowledge and skills for safe operation in all aspects of instrument flying. It should also prove very useful to pilots preparing for the instrument checkride or an instrument proficiency check—see a full version of this FAA guide on the "Reader Resource" webpage for this book.

You may supplement this guide with other study materials as noted in parentheses after each question; for example: (FAA-H-8083-15). The abbreviations for these materials and their titles are listed below. Be sure that you use the latest revision of these references when reviewing for the test. Also, check the ASA website at **www.asa2fly.com** for the latest updates to this book on our "Product Updates" page; all the latest changes in FAA procedures and regulations that affect these questions will be listed there.

| 14 CFR Part 61 | *Certification: Pilots, Flight Instructors, and Ground Instructors* |
| 14 CFR Part 91 | *General Operating and Flight Rules* |
| AC 00-6 | *Aviation Weather* |
| AC 00-45 | *Aviation Weather Services* |
| AIM | *Aeronautical Information Manual* |
| FAA-H-8083-9 | *Aviation Instructor's Handbook* |
| FAA-H-8083-15 | *Instrument Flying Handbook* |
| FAA-H-8083-25 | *Pilot's Handbook of Aeronautical Knowledge* |
| FAA-H-8261-1 | *Instrument Procedures Handbook* |
| FAA-S-8081-4 | *Instrument Rating Practical Test Standards* |
| P/CG | *Pilot/Controller Glossary included in the AIM* |

*All the books listed above are reprinted by ASA and are available from aviation retailers worldwide.*

| AC 00-54 | *Pilot Windshear Guide* |
|---|---|
| AC 61-65 | *Certification: Pilots, and Flight Instructors, and Ground Instructors* |
| AC 61-98 | *Currency and Additional Qualification Requirements for Certificated Pilots* |
| AC 61-126 | *Qualification and Approval of Personal Computer-Based Aviation Training Devices* |
| AC 90-94 | *Guidelines for Using Global Positioning Equipment for IFR En Route and Terminal Operations and for Nonprecision Instrument Approaches in the U.S. National Airspace System* |
| FAA-P-8740-16 | *Understanding and Caring for your Gyroscopic Instruments* |
| Order 7930.2 | *Notices to Airmen Handbook* |
| Order 8260.3B | *United States Standard for Terminal Instrument Procedures (TERPs)* |
| POH | *Pilot Operating Handbook* |
| AFM | *FAA Approved Flight Manual* |

*These advisory circulars are available from the Government Printing Office. POH/AFMs are available from the airplane manufacturer.*

A review of the information presented within this guide should provide the necessary preparation for the oral section of an FAA instrument certification or re-certification check.

Were you asked a question during your checkride that was not covered in this book? If so, please send the question to ASA. We are constantly striving to improve our publications to meet the industry needs.

email: asa@asa2fly.com
Fax: 425.235.0128

7005 132nd Place SE
Newcastle, WA 98059-3153

# Flight
# Planning

**1**

# A. Certificates, Ratings and Currency Requirements

## 1. An applicant for an instrument rating must have at least how much and what type of flight time as pilot? (14 CFR 61.65)

An applicant must have:

a. 50 hours of cross-country flight time as PIC, of which at least 10 hours must be in airplanes;

b. 40 hours of actual or simulated instrument time (on the areas of operation specified);

c. 15 hours of instrument flight training from an authorized instructor in the aircraft category for which the instrument rating is sought;

d. 3 hours of instrument training appropriate to the instrument rating sought from an authorized instructor, in preparation for the practical test, within the 60 days preceding the date of test;

e. 250 NM cross-country, conducted under IFR, including 3 different kinds of approaches.

## 2. When is an instrument rating required? (14 CFR 61.3e, 91.157)

When operations are conducted:

a. Under instrument flight rules (IFR flight plan),

b. In weather conditions less than the minimum for VFR flight,

c. In Class A airspace,

d. Under Special VFR within Class B, Class C, Class D and Class E surface areas between sunset and sunrise.

### 3. What are the recency-of-experience requirements to be PIC of a flight under IFR? (14 CFR 61.57)

The recency-of-experience requirements are:

a. A biennial flight review;

b. To carry passengers, 3 takeoffs and landings within the preceding 90 days (full stop at night);

c. Within the preceding 6 calendar months, logged under actual or simulated instrument conditions, either in flight in the appropriate category of aircraft, or in a flight simulator or flight training device (representative of the category for the privileges sought) —

   • At least six instrument approaches;

   • Holding procedures; and

   • Intercepting and tracking courses through the use of navigation systems.

### 4. If a pilot allows his/her instrument currency to expire, what can be done to become current again? (14 CFR 61.57, 91.109)

A pilot is current for the first 6 months following his/her instrument checkride or proficiency check. If the pilot has not accomplished at least 6 approaches (including holding procedures, intercepting/tracking courses through the use of navigation systems) within this first 6 months, he/she is no longer legal to file and fly under IFR. To become legal again, the regulations allow a "grace period" (the second 6-month period), in which a pilot may get current by finding an "appropriately rated" safety pilot, and in simulated IFR conditions only, acquire the 6 approaches, etc. If the second 6-month period also passes without accomplishing the minimum, a pilot may reinstate his/her currency by accomplishing an instrument proficiency check given by an examiner, an authorized instructor, or an FAA-approved person to conduct instrument practical tests.

5. **What are the required qualifications for a person to act as a "safety pilot"?** (14 CFR 61.3, 61.55, and 91.109)

The safety pilot must:

a. Possess a current medical certificate (the safety pilot is acting as a required crewmember).

b. Possess at least a private pilot certificate with category and class ratings appropriate to the aircraft being flown.

c. If the flight is to be conducted on an IFR flight plan, the safety pilot is also required to have an instrument rating (see 61.55(a)(2) second-in-command requirements).

# B. Preflight Action for Flight
(IFR or Flight Not in the Vicinity of Airport)

1. **What information must a pilot-in-command be familiar with before a flight?** (14 CFR 91.103)

All available information including:

a. Weather reports and forecasts

b. Fuel requirements

c. Alternatives if the flight cannot be completed as planned

d. Known ATC delays

e. Runway lengths of intended use

f. Takeoff and landing distances

2. **What are the fuel requirements for flight in IFR conditions?** (14 CFR 91.167)

The aircraft must carry enough fuel to fly to the first airport of intended landing (including the approach), the alternate airport (if required), and thereafter, for 45 minutes at normal cruise speed. If an alternate airport is not required, enough fuel must be carried to fly to the destination airport and land with 45 minutes of fuel remaining.

3. **Before conducting an IFR flight using GPS equipment for navigation, what basic preflight checks should be made?** (FAA-H-8261-1)

Preflight preparations should include:

a. Verify that the GPS equipment is properly installed and certified for the planned IFR operation.

b. Verify that the database is current and has not expired.

c. Review the GPS NOTAM/RAIM information for the planned route of flight.

# C. Preflight Action for Aircraft

1. **Who is responsible for determining if an aircraft is in an airworthy condition?** (14 CFR 91.7)

The pilot-in-command is responsible.

2. **What aircraft instruments/equipment are required for IFR operations?** (14 CFR 91.205)

Those required for VFR day and night flight plus:

**G** enerator or alternator of adequate capacity
**R** adios (nav equipment suitable for facilities used)
**A** ltimeter (sensitive)
**B** all (slip/skid indicator of turn coordinator)
**C** lock (sweep second hand or digital presentation)
**A** ttitude indicator
**R** ate of turn (turn coordinator)
**D** irectional gyro
**D** ME or RNAV (for flight at FL240 and above if VOR equipment is required for the route)

3. **What are the required tests and inspections of aircraft and equipment to be legal for IFR flight?**
(14 CFR 91.171, 91.409, 91.411 and 91.413)

a. The aircraft must have an annual inspection. If operated for hire or giving flight instruction for hire, it must also have a 100-hour inspection. A record must be kept in the aircraft/engine logbooks.

b. The pitot/static system must have been checked within the preceding 24 calendar months. A record must be kept in the aircraft logbook.

c. The transponder must have been checked within the preceding 24 calendar months. A record must be kept in the aircraft logbook.

d. The altimeter must have been checked within the preceding 24 calendar months. A record must be kept in the aircraft logbook.

e. The VOR must have been checked within the preceding 30 days. A record must be kept in a bound logbook.

f. ELT battery and inspection (12 calendar months).

**4. May portable electronic devices be operated on board an aircraft?** (14 CFR 91.21)

No person may operate nor may any PIC allow the operation of any portable electronic device:

a. On aircraft operated by an air carrier or commercial operator; or

b. On any other aircraft while it is operated under IFR.

Exceptions are: portable voice recorders, hearing aids, heart pacemakers, electric shavers or any other portable electronic device that the operator of the aircraft has determined will not cause interference with the navigation or communication system of the aircraft.

**5. What documents must be on board an aircraft to make it legal for IFR flight?** (14 CFR 91.9, 91.203)

**A** irworthiness Certificate
**R** egistration Certificate
**R** adio station license (if conducting international operations)
**O** wner's manual or operating limitations
**W** eight and balance data

**6. How often is the GPS waypoint information database updated?** (AC 90-94; FAA-H-8083-15)

Every 28 days, as provided and maintained by the National Flight Data Center (NFDC).

# D. IFR Flight Plan

## 1. When must a pilot file an IFR flight plan? (AIM 5-1-8)

Prior to departure from within or prior to entering controlled airspace, a pilot must submit a complete flight plan and receive clearance from ATC if weather conditions are below VFR minimums. The pilot should file the flight plan at least 30 minutes prior to the estimated time of departure to preclude a possible delay in receiving a departure clearance from ATC.

## 2. When can you cancel your IFR flight plan? (AIM 5-1-14)

An IFR flight plan may be canceled at any time the flight is operating in VFR conditions outside of Class A airspace. Pilots must be aware that other procedures may be applicable to a flight that cancels an IFR flight plan within an area where a special program, such as a designated TRSA, Class C airspace, or Class B airspace, has been established.

## 3. What is a composite flight plan? (AIM 5-1-7)

It is a flight plan that specifies VFR operation for one portion of a flight, and IFR for another.

## 4. What type of aircraft equipment determines your "special equipment" suffix when filing an IFR flight plan? (AIM 5-1-8)

a. Radar beacon transponder

b. DME equipment

c. TACAN-only equipment

d. Area Navigation equipment (RNAV)—LORAN, INS

e. Advanced Area Navigation equipment—Global Positioning System (GPS)/Global Navigation Satellite System (GNSS)

f. Reduced Vertical Separation Minimum (RVSM) authorization

## 5. The requested altitude on an FAA flight plan form (Block 7) represents which altitude for the route of flight—the initial, lowest, or highest? (AIM 5-1-8)

Enter only the initial requested altitude in this block. When more than one IFR altitude or flight level is desired along the route of flight, it is best to make a subsequent request direct to the controller.

## 6. What are the alternate airport requirements? (14 CFR 91.169c)

*1-2-3 Rule*—If from 1 hour before to 1 hour after your planned ETA at the destination airport, the weather is forecast to be at least 2,000-foot ceilings and 3-mile visibilities, no alternate is required. If less than 2,000 and 3 miles, an alternate must be filed using the following criteria:

a. If an IAP is published for that airport, the alternate airport minimums specified in that procedure or, if none are specified, the following minimums—

- Precision approach procedure: ceiling 600 feet and visibility 2 statute miles.
- Nonprecision approaches: ceiling 800 feet and visibility 2 statute miles.

b. If no IAP has been published for that airport, the ceiling and visibility minimums are those allowing descent from the MEA, approach, and landing under basic VFR.

## 7. What is the definition of the term "ceiling"? (P/CG)

Ceiling is defined as the height above the Earth's surface of the lowest layer of clouds or obscuring phenomena reported as "broken," "overcast," or "obscuration," and not classified as "thin" or "partial."

## 8. What minimums are to be used on arrival at the alternate? (14 CFR 91.169c)

If an instrument approach procedure has been published for that airport, the minimums specified in that procedure are used.

# E. Route Planning

### 1. What are preferred routes and where can they be found? (P/CG)

Preferred routes are those established between busier airports to increase system efficiency and capacity. Preferred routes are listed in the Airport/Facility Directory.

### 2. What are Enroute Low-Altitude Charts? (AIM 9-1-4)

Enroute low-altitude charts provide aeronautical information for navigation under IFR conditions below 18,000 feet MSL. These charts are revised every 56 days.

### 3. What are Enroute High-Altitude Charts? (AIM 9-1-4)

Enroute high-altitude charts are designed for navigation at or above 18,000 feet MSL. This four-color chart series includes the jet route structure; VHF NAVAIDs with frequency, identification, channel, geographic coordinates; selected airports; reporting points. Revised every 56 days.

### 4. What are "area charts"? (AIM 9-1-4)

Area charts show congested terminal areas such as Dallas/ Ft. Worth or Atlanta at a large scale. They are included with subscriptions to any conterminous U.S. set Low (Full set, East or West sets). Revised every 56 days.

### 5. Where can information on possible navigational aid limitations be found? (FAA-H-8083-15)

NOTAMs as well as A/FDs will contain current limitations to NAVAIDs.

## 6. What other useful information can be found in the Airport/Facility Directory which might be helpful in route planning? (A/FD)

The A/FD contains additional information for each of the seven regions covered, such as:

a. Enroute Flight Advisory Services—locations and communications outlets.

b. ARTCC—locations and sector frequencies.

c. Aeronautical Chart Bulletins—recent changes after publication.

d. Preferred IFR routes—high and low altitude.

e. Special notices—flight service station, GADO, Weather Service office phone numbers.

f. VOR receiver checkpoints—locations and frequencies.

## 7. What are NOTAMs? (AIM 5-1-3)

*Notices To Airmen* (NOTAM)—Time critical aeronautical information, which is of either a temporary nature or not known sufficiently in advance to permit publication on aeronautical charts or in other operational publications, receives immediate dissemination via the National NOTAM System. It is aeronautical information that could affect a pilot's decision to make a flight. It includes such information as airport or primary runway closures, changes in the status of navigational aids, ILS's, radar service availability, and other information essential to planned en route, terminal, or landing operations.

**8. What are the four groups of NOTAMs?** (Order 7930.2)

NOTAMs are classified into four groups:

a. *(D) NOTAMs* — Information that requires wide dissemination via telecommunication, regarding enroute navigational aids, civil public-use airports listed in the A/FD, facilities, services, and procedures.

b. *FDC NOTAMs* — Flight information that is regulatory in nature including, but not limited to, changes to IFR charts, procedures, and airspace usage.

c. *POINTER NOTAMs* — issued by a flight service station to highlight or point out another NOTAM; for example, an FDC NOTAM. These NOTAMs assist users in cross-referencing important information that may not be found under an airport or NAVAID identifier.

d. *MILITARY NOTAMs* — these pertain to U.S. Air Force, Army, Marine, and Navy navigational aids/airports that are part of the NAS.

**9. All (D) NOTAMs will have keywords contained within the first part of the text. What are several examples of these keywords?** (Order 7930.2)

RWY, TWY, RAMP, APRON, AD, OBST, NAV, COM, SVC, AIRSPACE, (U), or (O).

**10. Where can NOTAM information be obtained?** (AIM 5-1-3)

a. AFSS/FSS

b. DUATS vendors

c. NTAP printed NOTAMs; not normally a briefing. Pilots must make a specific request for them during briefing. The NTAP is also available online from the FAA's website.

**11. Will an FSS briefer provide GPS NOTAMs as part of a standard briefing?** (AIM 7-1-4)

No. A pilot must request GPS NOTAMs during a preflight briefing from an AFSS briefer.

# F. Flight Instruments

## Pitot/Static System

### 1. What instruments operate from the pitot/static system? (FAA-H-8083-15)

The pitot/static system operates the altimeter, vertical-speed indicator, and airspeed indicator.

### 2. How does an altimeter work? (FAA-H-8083-15)

In an altimeter, aneroid wafers expand and contract as atmospheric pressure changes, and through a shaft and gear linkage, rotate pointers on the dial of the instrument.

### 3. What are the limitations that a pressure altimeter is subject to? (FAA-H-8083-15)

Nonstandard pressure and temperature:

a. Temperature variations expand or contract the atmosphere and raise or lower pressure levels that the altimeter senses.

*On a warm day*—The pressure level is higher than on a standard day. The altimeter indicates lower than actual altitude.

*On a cold day*—The pressure level is lower than on a standard day. The altimeter indicates higher than actual altitude.

b. Changes in surface pressure also affect pressure levels at altitude.

*Higher than standard pressure*—The pressure level is higher than on a standard day. The altimeter indicates lower than actual altitude.

*Lower than standard pressure*—The pressure level is lower than on a standard day. The altimeter indicates higher than actual altitude.

***Remember:*** High to low or hot to cold look out below!

**4. For IFR flight, what is the maximum allowable error for an altimeter?** (FAA-H-8083-15)

If the altimeter is off field elevation by more than 75 feet, with the correct pressure set in the Kollsman window, it is considered to be unreliable.

**5. Define and state how to determine the following altitudes:**

| | |
|---|---|
| **Indicated altitude** | **Density altitude** |
| **Pressure altitude** | **Absolute altitude** |
| **True altitude** | |

(FAA-H-8083-25)

*Indicated altitude* — Read off the face of the altimeter.

*Pressure altitude* — Indicated altitude with 29.92" Hg set in the Kollsman window.

*True altitude* — Height above sea level. Use the flight computer.

*Density altitude* — Pressure altitude corrected for nonstandard temperature. Use the flight computer.

*Absolute altitude* — Height above ground. Subtract the terrain elevation from true altitude.

**6. How does the airspeed indicator operate?** (FAA-H-8083-15)

The airspeed indicator measures the difference between ram pressure from the pitot head and atmospheric pressure from the static source.

**7. What are the limitations the airspeed indicator is subject to?** (FAA-H-8083-15)

It must have proper flow of air in the pitot/static system.

## 8. What are the errors that the airspeed indicator is subject to?

*Position error*—caused by the static ports sensing erroneous static pressure; slipstream flow causes disturbances at the static port preventing actual atmospheric pressure measurement. It varies with airspeed, altitude, configuration and may be a plus or minus value.

*Density error*—changes in altitude and temperature are not compensated for by the instrument.

*Compressibility error*—caused by the packing of air into the pitot tube at high airspeeds, resulting in higher than normal indications. It usually occurs above 180 KIAS.

## 9. What are the different types of aircraft speeds?
(FAA-H-8083-15)

*Indicated Airspeed (IAS)*—the speed of the airplane read off the airspeed indicator, without correction for indicator, position (or installation), or compressibility errors.

*Calibrated Airspeed (CAS)*—the airspeed indicator reading corrected for position (or installation), and instrument errors; equal to TAS at sea level in standard atmosphere. The color-coding for various design speeds marked on airspeed indicators may be IAS or CAS.

*Equivalent Airspeed (EAS)*—the AS reading corrected for position (or installation), or instrument error, and for adiabatic compressible flow for the particular altitude; equal to CAS at sea level in standard atmosphere.

*True Airspeed (TAS)*—the speed of the airplane in relation to the air mass in which it is flying.

## 10. What airspeeds are indicated by the various color codes found on the dial of an airspeed indicator? (FAA-H-8083-25)

White arc................................................................flap operating range

Bottom of white arc ......................................flaps down stall speed

Top of white arc ...............maximum airspeed for flaps-down flight

Green arc................................................................normal operating range

Bottom of green arc ............................................flaps up stall speed

Top of green arc ...........................maximum airspeed for rough air

Yellow arc ..................................................structural warning area

Bottom of yellow arc ....................maximum airspeed for rough air

Top of yellow arc ...........................................never-exceed airspeed

Red radial line................................................never-exceed airspeed

## 11. How does the vertical-speed indicator work? (FAA-H-8083-15)

In the VSI, changing pressures expand or contract a diaphragm connected to the indicating needle through gears and levers. The VSI is connected to the static pressure line through a calibrated leak; it measures differential pressure.

## 12. What are the limitations of the vertical-speed indicator? (FAA-H-8083-15)

It is not accurate until the aircraft is stabilized. Sudden or abrupt changes in the aircraft attitude will cause erroneous instrument readings as airflow fluctuates over the static port. These changes are not reflected immediately by the VSI due to the calibrated leak.

## 13. What instruments are affected when the pitot tube ram air inlet and drain hole freeze? (FAA-H-8083-25)

Only the airspeed indicator will be affected. It acts like an altimeter—it will read higher as the aircraft climbs and lower as the aircraft descends. It reads lower than actual speed in level flight.

## 14. What instruments are affected when the static port freezes? (FAA-H-8083-25)

*Airspeed indicator*—Accurate at the altitude frozen as long as static pressure in the indicator and the system equals outside pressure. If the aircraft descends, the airspeed indicator would read high (outside static pressure would be greater than that trapped). If the aircraft climbs, the airspeed indicator would read low.

*Altimeter*—Indicates the altitude at which the system is blocked.

*Vertical speed*—Will indicate level flight.

## 15. If the air temperature is +6°C at an airport elevation of 1,200 feet and a standard (average) temperature lapse rate exists, what will be the approximate freezing level?

4,200 MSL; 6° at the surface divided by the average temperature lapse rate of 2°C results in a 3,000-foot freezing level, converted to sea level by adding the 1,200-foot airport elevation.

## 16. What corrective action is needed if the pitot tube freezes? If the static port freezes? (FAA-H-8083-15)

*For pitot tube*—Turn pitot heat on.

*For static system*—Use alternate air if available or break the face of a static instrument (either the VSI or A/S indicator).

## 17. What indications should you expect while using alternate air? (FAA-H-8083-25)

In many unpressurized aircraft equipped with a pitot-static tube, an alternate source of static pressure is provided for emergency use. If the alternate source is vented inside the airplane where static pressure is usually lower than outside, selection of the alternate static source may result in the following indications:

| | |
|---|---|
| Altimeter | will indicate higher than the actual altitude |
| Airspeed | will indicate greater than the actual airspeed |
| Vertical speed | will indicate a climb while in level flight |

*Note: Always consult the AFM/POH to determine the amount of error.*

### Gyroscopic System

### 1. What instruments contain gyroscopes? (FAA-H-8083-15)

Attitude indicator, heading indicator and turn coordinator/indicator.

### 2. Name several types of power sources commonly used to power the gyroscopic instruments in an aircraft. (FAA-H-8083-15)

Various power sources used are: electrical, pneumatic, venturi tube, wet-type vacuum pump, and dry-air pump systems. Aircraft and instrument manufacturers have designed redundancy into the flight instruments so that any single failure will not deprive the pilot of his/her ability to safely conclude the flight. Gyroscopic instruments are crucial for instrument flight; therefore, they are powered by separate electrical or pneumatic sources. Typically, the heading indicator and attitude indicator will be vacuum-driven and the turn coordinator electrically-driven.

*Note:* It is extremely important that pilots consult the POH/AFM to determine the power source of all instruments to know what action to take in the event of an instrument failure.

### 3. How does the vacuum system operate? (FAA-H-8083-25)

The vacuum or pressure system spins the gyro by drawing a stream of air against the rotor vanes to spin the rotor at high speeds, essentially the same as a water wheel or turbine operates. The amount of vacuum or pressure required for instrument operation varies by manufacturer and is usually between 4.5 to 5.5 in. Hg. One source of vacuum for the gyros installed in light aircraft is the vane-type engine-driven pump, mounted on the accessory case of the engine.

### 4. What are two important characteristics of gyroscopes? (FAA-H-8083-15)

*Rigidity*—the characteristic of a gyro that prevents its axis of rotation tilting as the Earth rotates; attitude and heading instruments operate on this principle.

*Precession*—the characteristic of a gyro that causes an applied force to be felt, not at the point of application, but 90 degrees from that point in the direction of rotation. Rate instruments such as the turn coordinator use this principle.

## 5. How does the turn coordinator operate? (FAA-H-8083-15)

The turn part of the instrument uses precession to indicate direction and approximate rate of turn. A gyro reacts by trying to move in reaction to the force applied, thus moving the miniature aircraft in proportion to the rate of turn. The inclinometer in the instrument is a black glass ball sealed inside a curved glass tube that is partially filled with a liquid. The ball measures the relative strength of the force of gravity and the force of inertia caused by a turn.

## 6. What information does the turn coordinator provide? (FAA-H-8083-15)

The miniature aircraft in the turn coordinator displays the rate of turn, rate of roll and direction of turn. The ball in the tube indicates the quality of turn (slip or skid).

*Slip*—ball on the inside of turn; not enough rate of turn for the amount of bank.

*Skid*—ball to the outside of turn; too much rate of turn for the amount of bank.

## 7. What is the source of power for the turn coordinator? (FAA-H-8083-15)

Turn coordinator gyros can be driven by either air or electricity; some are dual-powered. Typically the turn coordinator is electrically powered, but always refer to the AFM for specifics.

## 8. How does the heading indicator work? (FAA-H-8083-25)

The operation of the heading indicator works on the principle of rigidity in space. The rotor turns in a vertical plane, and fixed to the rotor is a compass card. Since the rotor remains rigid in space, the points on the card hold the same position in space relative to the vertical plane. As the instrument case and the airplane revolve around the vertical axis, the card provides clear and accurate heading information.

### 9. What are the limitations of the heading indicator? (FAA-H-8083-25)

They vary with the particular design and make of instrument: on some heading indicators in light airplanes, the limits are approximately 55 degrees of pitch and 55 degrees of bank. When either of these attitude limits are exceeded, the instrument "tumbles" or "spills" and no longer gives the correct indication until it is reset with the caging knob. Many modern instruments used are designed in such a manner that they will not tumble.

### 10. What type of error is the heading indicator subject to? (FAA-H-8083-25)

Because of precession (caused by friction), the heading indicator will creep or drift from the heading it is set to. The amount of drift depends largely upon the condition of the instrument (worn and dirty bearings and/or improperly lubricated bearings). Additionally, the gyro is oriented in space and the earth rotates in space at a rate of 15 degrees in 1 hour; therefore, discounting precession caused by friction, the heading indicator may indicate as much as 15 degrees of error per every hour of operation.

### 11. How does the attitude indicator work? (FAA-H-8083-25)

The gyro in the attitude indicator is mounted on a horizontal plane and depends upon rigidity in space for its operation. The horizon bar represents the true horizon and is fixed to the gyro; it remains in a horizontal plane as the airplane is pitched or banked about its lateral or longitudinal axis, indicating the attitude of the airplane relative to the true horizon.

## 12. What are the limitations of an attitude indicator?
(FAA-H-8083-25)

Limits depend upon the make and model of the instrument; bank limits are usually from 100° to 110°, and pitch limits are usually from 60° to 70°. If either limit is exceeded, the instrument will tumble or spill and will give incorrect indications until restabilized. Some modern attitude indicators are designed so they will not tumble.

## 13. Is the attitude indicator subject to errors?
(FAA-H-8083-15)

Attitude indicators are free from most errors, but depending upon the speed with which the erection system functions, there may be a slight nose-up indication during a rapid acceleration and a nose-down indication during a rapid deceleration. There is also a possibility of a small bank angle and pitch error after a 180° turn. On rollout from a 180° turn, the AI will indicate a slight climb and turn in the opposite direction of rollout. These inherent errors are small and correct themselves within a minute or so after returning to straight-and-level flight.

## Magnetic Compass

### 1. How does the magnetic compass work? (FAA-H-8083-15)

Magnets mounted on the compass card align themselves parallel to the Earth's lines of magnetic force.

### 2. What limitations does the magnetic compass have? (FAA-H-8083-15)

The jewel-and-pivot type mounting gives the float freedom to rotate and tilt up to approximately 18° angle of bank. At steeper bank angles, the compass indications are erratic and unpredictable.

### 3. What are the various compass errors? (FAA-H-8083-15)

*Oscillation error*—Erratic movement of the compass card caused by turbulence or rough control technique.

*Deviation error*—Due to electrical and magnetic disturbances in the aircraft.

*Variation error*—Angular difference between true and magnetic north; reference isogonic lines of variation.

*Dip errors:*

a. *Acceleration error*—On east or west headings, while accelerating, the magnetic compass shows a turn to the north, and when decelerating, it shows a turn to the south.

   *Remember:* ANDS
   **A** ccelerate
   **N** orth
   **D** ecelerate
   **S** outh

b. *Northerly turning error*—The compass leads in the south half of a turn, and lags in the north half of a turn.

   *Remember:* UNOS
   **U** ndershoot
   **N** orth
   **O** vershoot
   **S** outh

# G. Fundamentals of Weather

**1. At what rate does atmospheric pressure decrease with an increase in altitude?** (AC 00-6A)

Atmospheric pressure decreases approximately 1" Hg per 1,000 feet.

**2. What are the standard temperature and pressure values for sea level?** (AC 00-6A)

15°C and 29.92" Hg are standard at sea level.

**3. State the general characteristics in regard to the flow of air around high and low pressure systems in the northern hemisphere.** (AC 00-6A)

*Low pressure* — Air flows inward, upward, and counterclockwise.

*High pressure* — Air flows outward, downward, and clockwise.

**4. What causes the winds aloft to flow parallel to the isobars?** (AC 00-6A)

The Coriolis force causes winds aloft to flow parallel to the isobars.

**5. Why do surface winds generally flow across the isobars at an angle?** (AC 00-6A)

Surface friction causes winds to flow across isobars at an angle.

**6. When temperature and dew point are close together (within 5°), what type of weather is likely?** (AC 00-6A)

Visible moisture is likely, in the form of clouds, dew or fog.

**7. What factor primarily determines the type and vertical extent of clouds?** (AC 00-6A)

The stability of the atmosphere determines type and vertical extent of clouds.

8. **What is the difference between a stable and an unstable atmosphere?** (AC 00-6A)

   A stable atmosphere resists any upward or downward displacement. An unstable atmosphere allows an upward or downward disturbance to grow into a vertical or convective current.

9. **How do you determine the stability of the atmosphere?** (AC 00-6A)

   When temperature decreases uniformly and rapidly as you climb (approaching 3°C per 1,000 feet), you have an indication of unstable air. If the temperature remains unchanged or decreases only slightly with altitude, the air tends to be stable. When air near the surface is warm and moist, suspect instability.

10. **List the effects of stable and unstable air on clouds, turbulence, precipitation and visibility.** (AC 00-6A)

    |  | **Stable** | **Unstable** |
    |---|---|---|
    | Clouds | Stratiform | Cumuliform |
    | Turbulence | Smooth | Rough |
    | Precipitation | Steady | Showery |
    | Visibility | Fair to Poor | Good |

11. **What are the main types of icing an aircraft may encounter?** (AC 00-6A)

    Structural, induction system, and instrument icing.

12. **Name the three types of structural ice.** (AC 00-6A)

    *Clear ice*—Forms when large drops strike the aircraft surface and slowly freeze.

    *Rime ice*—Small drops strike the aircraft and freeze rapidly.

    *Mixed ice*—Combination of the above; supercooled water drops varying in size, intermingled with snow or ice particles, building a rough accumulation.

**13. What are the intensity categories of aircraft structural icing?** (AC 00-45)

a. *Trace* — ice becomes perceptible; rate of accumulation slightly greater than sublimation; deicing/anti-icing equipment is not used unless encountered for extended period of time (over 1 hour).

b. *Light* — rate of accumulation may create a problem if flight is prolonged in this environment (over 1 hour). Occasional use of deicing/anti-icing equipment removes or prevents accumulation.

c. *Moderate* — the rate of accumulation is such that even short encounters become potentially hazardous; use of deicing/anti-icing equipment or diversion is necessary.

d. *Severe* — rate of accumulation is such that deicing/anti-icing equipment fails to reduce or control the hazard; immediate diversion is necessary.

**14. What is the definition of the term freezing level and how can you determine where that level is?** (AC 00-6A)

The freezing level is the lowest altitude in the atmosphere over a given location at which the air temperature reaches 0°C. It is possible to have multiple freezing layers when a temperature inversion occurs above the defined freezing level. A pilot should use icing forecasts as well as PIREPs to determine the approximate freezing level. Area forecasts, AIRMETs, SIGMETs, and Low-Level Significant Weather Charts are several examples of aviation weather products that contain icing information.

**15. What factors must be present for a thunderstorm to form?** (AC 00-6A)

To form a thunderstorm there must be:

a. A source of lift (heating, fast-moving front)

b. Unstable air (nonstandard lapse rate)

c. High moisture content (temperature and dew point are close).

## 16. What are "squall line" thunderstorms? (AC 00-6A)

A squall line is a non-frontal, narrow band of active thunderstorms. Often it develops ahead of a cold front in moist, unstable air, but it may also develop in unstable air far removed from any front. The line may be too long to easily detour and too wide and severe to penetrate. It often contains severe steady-state thunderstorms and presents the single most intense weather hazard to aircraft. It usually forms rapidly, reaching a maximum intensity during the late afternoon and the first few hours of darkness.

## 17. State two basic ways that fog may form. (AC 00-6A)

Fog forms:

a. By cooling air to the dew point

b. By adding moisture to the air

## 18. Name several types of fog. (AC 00-6A)

a. Radiation fog

b. Advection fog

c. Upslope fog

d. Precipitation-induced fog

e. Ice fog

## 19. What causes radiation fog to form? (AC 00-6A)

Conditions favorable for radiation fog are a clear sky, little or no wind, and small temperature-dew point spread (high relative humidity). The fog forms almost exclusively at night or near daybreak.

## 20. What is advection fog, and where is it most likely to form? (AC 00-6A)

Advection fog forms when moist air moves over colder ground or water. It is most common along coastal areas but often develops deep in continental areas. Unlike radiation fog, it may occur with winds, cloudy skies, over a wide geographic area, and at any time of the day or night. It deepens as wind speed increases up to about 15 knots; wind much stronger than 15 knots lifts the fog into a layer of low stratus or stratocumulus.

### 21. Define upslope fog. (AC 00-6A)

Upslope fog forms as a result of moist, stable air being cooled adiabatically as it moves up sloping terrain. Once the upslope wind ceases, the fog dissipates. Unlike radiation fog, it can form under cloudy skies. It is common along the eastern slopes of the Rockies and somewhat less frequent east of the Appalachians; can often be quite dense and extend to high altitudes.

### 22. Define ice fog. (AC 00-6A)

Ice fog occurs in cold weather when the temperature is much below freezing and water vapor sublimates directly as ice crystals. Conditions favorable for its formation are the same as for radiation fog except for cold temperature, usually -25°F or colder. It occurs mostly in the Arctic regions, but is not unknown in middle latitudes during the cold season. Ice fog can be quite blinding to someone flying into the sun.

### 23. What is precipitation-induced fog? (AC 00-6A)

When relatively warm rain or drizzle falls through cool air, evaporation from the precipitation saturates the cool air and forms fog. Precipitation-induced fog can become quite dense and continue for an extended period of time. This fog may extend over large areas, completely suspending air operations. It is most commonly associated with warm fronts, but can occur with slow-moving cold fronts and with stationary fronts.

### 24. Other than fog, what are several other examples of IFR weather producers? (AC 00-6A)

Other examples of common IFR producers are low clouds (stratus), haze, smoke, blowing obstructions to vision, and precipitation. Fog and low stratus restrict navigation by visual reference more often than all other weather phenomena.

# H. Obtaining Weather Information

### 1. What is the primary means of obtaining a weather briefing? (AIM 7-1-2)

The primary source of preflight weather briefings is an individual briefing obtained from a briefer at the AFSS/FSS.

### 2. What are some examples of other sources of weather information? (AIM 7-1-2)

a. Telephone Information Briefing Service (TIBS) (AFSS)

b. Weather and aeronautical information from numerous private industries sources

c. The Direct User Access Terminal System (DUATS)

d. In Alaska, Transcribed Weather Broadcast (TWEB) and telephone access to the TWEB (TEL-TWEB)

### 3. What pertinent information should a weather briefing include? (AIM 7-1-4)

a. Adverse conditions

b. VFR flight not recommended

c. Synopsis

d. Current conditions

e. Enroute forecast

f. Destination forecast

g. Winds aloft

h. Notices to Airmen (NOTAMs)

i. ATC delay

In addition, upon request pilots may obtain the following from AFSS/FSS briefers: Information on Special Use Airspace (SUA), SUA related airspace and MTR activity within the flight plan area and a 100 NM extension around the flight plan area, a review of printed NOTAM publications, approximate density altitude data, information on air traffic services and rules, customs/immigration procedures, ADIZ rules, search and rescue, LORAN-C NOTAMs, available military NOTAMs, and runway friction measurement value NOTAMs, GPS RAIM availability, and other assistance as required.

### 4. What is "EFAS"? (AIM 7-1-5)

Enroute Flight Advisory Service (EFAS) is a service specifically designed to provide enroute aircraft with timely and meaningful weather advisories pertinent to the type of flight intended, route of flight, and altitude. EFAS is also a central collection and distribution point for pilot-reported weather information (PIREPs). EFAS provides communications capabilities for aircraft flying at 5,000 feet above ground level to 17,500 feet MSL on a common frequency of 122.0 MHz. It is also known as "Flight Watch." Discrete EFAS frequencies have been established to ensure communications coverage from 18,000 through 45,000 feet MSL, serving in each specific ARTCC area. These discrete frequencies may be used below 18,000 feet when coverage permits reliable communication.

### 5. What is "HIWAS"? (AIM 7-1-10)

Hazardous In-flight Weather Advisory Service (HIWAS) is a continuous broadcast of in-flight weather advisories including summarized Aviation Weather Warnings, SIGMETs, Convective SIGMETs, Center Weather Advisories, AIRMETs, and urgent PIREPs. HIWAS is an additional source of hazardous weather information which makes this data available on a continuous basis.

# I. Aviation Weather Reports and Observations

### 1. What is a METAR? (AC 00-45)

The aviation routine weather report (METAR) is the weather observer's interpretation of the weather conditions at a given site and time. There are two types of METAR reports: a routine METAR report that is transmitted every hour and an aviation selected special weather report (SPECI). This is a special report that can be given at any time to update the METAR for rapidly changing weather conditions, aircraft mishaps, or other critical information.

## 2. Describe the basic elements of a METAR. (AC 00-45)

A METAR report contains the following elements in the order presented:

a. *Type of report*—the METAR (routine), and SPECI (special observation).

b. *Station identifier*—(ICAO) four-letter station identifier; in the conterminous United States, the three-letter identifier is pre-fixed with K.

c. *Date and time of report*—six-digit date/time group appended with Z to denote Coordinated Universal Time (UTC). The first two digits are the date followed with two digits for hour and two digits for minutes.

d. *Modifier (as required)*—if used AUTO identifies a METAR/SPECI report as an automated weather report with no human intervention.

e. *Wind*—five-digit group (six digits if speed is over 99 knots); first three digits, direction of the wind from in tens of degrees referenced to true north. Directions less than 100 degrees are preceded with a zero; next two digits are average speed in knots, measured or estimated, or if over 99 knots, the next three digits.

f. *Visibility*—prevailing visibility in statute miles followed by a space, fractions of statute miles, as needed, and the letters SM.

g. *Runway visual range (RVR) (as required)*—follows the visibility element.

h. *Weather phenomena*—broken into two categories: qualifiers and weather phenomena.

i. *Sky condition*—reported in the following format: Amount/Height/Type (as required) or Indefinite Ceiling/Height (Vertical Visibility)

j. *Temperature/dew point group*—two-digit form in whole degrees Celsius separated by a solidus (/). Temperatures below zero are prefixed with M.

k. *Altimeter*—four-digit format representing tens, units, tenths, and hundredths of inches of mercury prefixed with an "A." The decimal point is not reported or stated.

1. *Remarks (RMK) (as required)* — operational significant weather phenomena, location of phenomena, beginning and ending times, direction of movement.

Example:   METAR KLAX 140651Z AUTO 00000KT 1SM
           R35L/4500V6000FT -RA BR BKN030 10/10 A2990
           RMK AO2

The following is an example of the phraseology used to relay this report to a pilot. Optional words or phrases are shown in parentheses: Los Angeles (California) (zero six five one observation), wind calm, visibility one, runway three five left RVR, variable between four thousand five hundred and six thousand feet, light rain, mist, broken ceiling 3,000 feet, temperature ten, dew point ten, altimeter two niner niner zero.

## 3. What are several types of weather observing programs? (AIM 7-1-12)

a. *Manual observations* — Reports made from airport locations staffed by FAA or NWS personnel.

b. *AWOS* — Automated Weather Observing System, which consists of various sensors, a processor, a computer-generated voice sub-system, and a transmitter to broadcast local, minute-by-minute weather data directly to the pilot. Observations include the prefix "AUTO" in the data.

c. *AWOS Broadcasts* — Computer-generated voice is used to automate the broadcast of minute-by-minute weather observations.

d. *ASOS/AWSS* — Automated Surface Observing System/ Automated Weather Sensor System, the primary U.S. surface weather observing system. AWSS is a follow-on program that provides identical data as ASOS. The system provides continuous minute-by-minute observations generating METARs and other aviation weather information, transmitted over a discrete VHF radio frequency or the voice portion of a local NAVAID.

### 4. What are PIREPs (UA), and where are they usually found? (AC 00-45)

An abbreviation for "pilot weather reports." A report of meteorological phenomena encountered by aircraft in flight. Required elements for all PIREPs are type of report, location, time, flight level, aircraft type, and at least one weather element encountered. All altitude references are MSL unless otherwise noted. Distance for visibility is in SM; all other distances are in NM. Time is in UTC. The two types of PIREPs are the routine (UA) and the urgent (UUA).

### 5. What are radar weather reports? (AC 00-45)

A radar weather report (SD/ROB) contains information about precipitation observed by weather radar. It is a textual product derived from the WSR-88D NEXRAD radar without human intervention. Reports are transmitted hourly and contain the following: location ID, time, configuration (CELL, LN, and AREA), coverage, precipitation type and intensity, location, maximum tops, cell movement, and remarks. The resolution of an SD/ROB is very coarse, up to 80 minutes old, and should only be used if no other radar information is available.

# J. Aviation Weather Forecasts

## 1. What are terminal aerodrome forecasts (TAFs)?
(AC 00-45, AIM 7-1-30)

It is a concise statement of the expected meteorological conditions within a 5 SM radius from the center of an airport's runway complex during a 24-hour time period. TAFs use the same weather code found in METAR weather reports, in the following format:

a. *Type of reports* — a routine forecast (TAF); and an amended forecast, TAF AMD.

b. *ICAO station identifier* — 4-letter station identifiers.

c. *Date and time of origin* — the date and UTC for when the forecast was actually prepared, in ICAO format. Valid time, TEMPOs and PROBs are presented ddhh/ddhh, FROM groups are presented ddhhmm.

d. *Valid period date and time* — valid forecast period is a 2-digit date followed by the 2-digit beginning and 2-digit ending hours in UTC. Routine TAFs are valid for 24 hours and are issued four times daily at 0000Z, 0600Z, 1200Z, and 1800Z.

e. *Forecasts* — wind, visibility, significant weather, sky condition, nonconvective low-level wind shear, change indicators, probability.

*Note:* The TAF date and time format recently changed to conform to ICAO standards. This change provides 30-hour TAFs for 32 high-impact U.S. airports. The remainder of TAF reporting stations will continue with 24-hour forecasts. The date and time format of all TAFs changed to accommodate the extended TAF period as detailed in item c. above.

## 2. What is an aviation area forecast? (AC 00-45)

A forecast of visual meteorological conditions (VMC), clouds, and general weather conditions over an area the size of several states. Must be used along with inflight weather advisories to determine forecast enroute weather and to interpolate conditions at airports where no TAFs are issued, in order to understand the complete weather picture. FAs are issued 3 times a day by the Aviation Weather Center (AWC) for each of the 6 areas in the contiguous 48 states.

### 3. What information is provided by an aviation area forecast? (AC 00-45)

Area forecasts (abbreviated "FA") are issued for the conterminous U.S. and cover the airspace between the surface and 45,000 feet AMSL. They include:

a. Synopsis: brief discussion of the synoptic weather affecting the FA area during the 18-hour valid period.

b. Clouds and weather: description of the clouds and weather for the first 12-hour period for each state or group of states, including:

   • Cloud amount (SCT, BKN or OVC) for clouds with bases higher than or equal to 1,000 feet AGL and below FL180,

   • Cloud bases and tops (AMSL) associated with the above,

   • Precipitation,

   • Visibilities between 3 and 6 SM and obstruction(s) to visibility,

   • Sustained surface winds 20 knots or greater.

c. 12- to 18-hour categorical outlook: IFR, marginal VFR (MVFR), or VFR, including expected precipitation and/or obstruction(s) to visibility.

### 4. What are In-flight Aviation Weather Advisories (WST, WS, WA)? (AIM 7-1-6)

Forecasts that advise enroute aircraft of development of potentially hazardous weather. All heights are referenced MSL, except in the case of ceilings (CIG) which indicates AGL. The advisories are of three types: convective SIGMET (WST), SIGMET (WS), and AIRMET (WA).

## 5. What is a convective SIGMET? (AIM 7-1-6)

A convective SIGMET (WST) implies severe or greater turbulence, severe icing and low-level wind shear. It may be issued for any convective situation which the forecaster feels is hazardous to all categories of aircraft. Convective SIGMET bulletins are issued for the Eastern (E), Central (C) and Western (W) United States (convective SIGMETs are not issued for Alaska or Hawaii). Bulletins are issued hourly at H+55. Special bulletins are issued at any time as required and updated at H+55. The text of the bulletin consists of either an observation and a forecast, or just a forecast, which is valid for up to 2 hours.

a. Severe thunderstorm due to:
  - Surface winds greater than or equal to 50 knots
  - Hail at the surface greater than or equal to 3/4 inches in diameter
  - Tornadoes

b. Embedded thunderstorms

c. A line of thunderstorms

d. Thunderstorms producing greater than or equal to heavy precipitation that affects 40 percent or more of an area at least 3,000 square miles.

## 6. What is a SIGMET? (AIM 7-1-6)

A SIGMET (WS) advises of non-convective weather that is potentially hazardous to all aircraft. SIGMETs are issued for the six areas corresponding to the FA areas. The maximum forecast period is four hours. In the conterminous United States, SIGMETs are issued when the following phenomena occur or are expected to occur:

a. Severe icing not associated with a thunderstorm.

b. Severe or extreme turbulence or clear air turbulence (CAT) not associated with thunderstorms.

c. Dust storms or sandstorms lowering surface or in-flight visibilities to below 3 miles.

d. Volcanic ash.

### 7. What is an AIRMET? (AIM 7-1-6)

AIRMETs (abbreviated "WA") are advisories of significant weather phenomena that describe conditions at intensities lower than those which require the issuance of SIGMETs, intended for use by all pilots in the preflight and enroute phase of flight to enhance safety. AIRMET bulletins are issued every 6 hours beginning at 0145 UTC during Central Daylight Time and at 0245 UTC during Central Standard Time. Each AIRMET includes an outlook for conditions expected after the AIRMET valid period, and contain details about IFR, extensive mountain obscuration, turbulence, strong surface winds, icing, and freezing levels.

### 8. What are the different types of AIRMETs? (AIM 7-1-6)

There are three AIRMETs—Sierra, Tango, and Zulu:

a.  AIRMET Sierra describes IFR conditions and/or extensive mountain obscurations.

b.  AIRMET Tango describes moderate turbulence, sustained surface winds of 30 knots or greater, and/or nonconvective low-level wind shear.

c.  AIRMET Zulu describes moderate icing and provides freezing level heights.

### 9. What is a winds and temperatures aloft forecast (FB)? (AC 00-45)

Winds and temperature aloft forecasts are computer prepared forecasts of wind direction, wind speed, and temperature at specified times, altitudes, and locations. They are produced 4 times daily for specified locations in the continental United States, Hawaii, Alaska and coastal waters, and the western Pacific Ocean. Amendments are not issued to the forecasts. Wind forecasts are not issued for altitudes within 1,500 feet of a location's elevation.

Some of the features of FBs are:

a.  Product header includes date and time observations collected, forecast valid date and time, and the time period during which the forecast is to be used.

b.  Altitudes up to 15,000 feet referenced to MSL; altitudes at or above 18,000 feet are references to flight levels (FL).

c. Temperature indicated in degrees Celsius (two digits) for the levels from 6,000 through 24,000 feet. Above 24,000 feet, minus sign is omitted since temperatures are always negative at those altitudes. Temperature forecasts are not issued for altitudes within 2,500 feet of a location's elevation. Forecasts for intermediate levels are determined by interpolation.

d. Wind direction indicated in tens of degrees (two digits) with reference to true north and wind speed is given in knots (two digits). Light and variable wind or wind speeds of less than 5 knots are expressed by 9900. Forecast wind speeds of 100 through 199 knots are indicated by subtracting 100 from the speed and adding 50 to the coded direction. For example, a forecast of 250 degrees, 145 knots, is encoded as 7545. Forecast wind speeds of 200 knots or greater are indicated as a forecast speed of 199 knots. For example, 7799 is decoded as 270 degrees at 199 knots or greater.

## 10. What valuable information can be determined from a winds and temperatures aloft forecast?

*Most favorable altitude* — based on winds and direction of flight.

*Areas of possible icing* — by noting air temperatures of +2°C to -20°C.

*Temperature inversions.*

*Turbulence* — by observing abrupt changes in wind direction and speed at different altitudes.

## 11. What is a Center Weather Advisory (CWA)? (AC 00-45)

A Center Weather Advisory (CWA) is an aviation warning for use by aircrews to anticipate and avoid adverse weather conditions in the en route and terminal environments. This is not a flight planning product; instead it reflects current conditions expected at the time of issuance, and/or is a short-range forecast for conditions expected to begin within 2 hours from that time. CWAs are valid for a maximum of 2 hours. If conditions are expected to continue beyond that period, a statement will be included in the CWA.

# K. Aviation Weather Charts

### 1. Give some examples of current weather charts, which are used in flight planning and available at the FSS or NWSO. (AC 00-45)

   a.  Surface Analysis Chart

   b.  Weather Depiction Chart

   c.  Radar Summary Chart

   d.  Significant Weather Prognostic Chart

   e.  Short-Range Surface Prognostic Chart

   f.  Convective Outlook Chart

   g.  Constant Pressure Analysis Chart

### 2. What is a surface analysis chart? (AC 00-45)

The surface analysis chart is a computer-prepared chart that covers the contiguous 48 states and adjacent areas. The chart is transmitted every three hours. The surface analysis chart provides a ready means of locating pressure systems and fronts. It also gives an overview of winds, temperatures and dew point temperatures at chart time. When using the chart, keep in mind that weather moves and conditions change. Using the surface analysis chart in conjunction with other information gives a more complete weather picture.

### 3. What information does a weather depiction chart provide? (AC 00-45)

This chart is computer-generated (with frontal analysis by an observer) from METAR reports, and gives a broad overview of the observed flying category conditions at the valid time of the chart. It begins at 01Z each day, is transmitted at 3-hours intervals, and is valid at the time of the plotted data. Observations reported by both manual and automated observation locations provide the following data: total sky cover, cloud height, weather and obstructions to visibility, visibility. The weather depiction chart is an ideal place to begin preparing for a weather briefing and flight planning. From this chart, one can get a "bird's-eye-view" of areas of favorable and adverse weather conditions for chart time.

## 4. Define the terms: LIFR, IFR, MVFR and VFR. (AIM 7-1-7)

LIFR   *Low IFR: ceiling less than 500 feet and/or visibility less than 1 mile*

IFR   *Ceiling 500 to less than 1,000 feet and/or visibility 1 to less than 3 miles*

MVFR   *Marginal VFR: ceiling 1,000 to 3,000 feet and/or visibility 3 to 5 miles inclusive*

VFR   *Ceiling greater than 3,000 feet and visibility greater than 5 miles; includes sky clear*

## 5. What are radar summary charts? (AC 00-45)

This chart is a computer-generated graphical display of a collection of automated radar weather reports (SDs, or ROBs), displaying areas of precipitation as well as information about type, intensity, configuration, coverage, echo top, and cell movement of precipitation. Severe weather watches are plotted if they are in effect when the chart is valid. It is available hourly with a valid time 35 minutes past each hour.

This chart aids in preflight planning by identifying general areas and movement of precipitation and/or thunderstorms. It displays drops or ice particles of precipitation size only; it does not display clouds and fog. Therefore, since the absence of echoes does not guarantee clear weather, and cloud tops will most likely be higher than the tops of the precipitation echoes detected by radar, the radar summary chart must be used in conjunction with other charts, reports, and forecasts for best effectiveness.

## 6. What are Short-Range Surface Prognostic charts? (AC 00-45)

Short-Range Surface Prognostic (Prog) Charts provide a forecast of surface pressure systems, fronts and precipitation for a 2-day period. The forecast area covers the 48-contiguous states, the coastal waters and portions of adjacent countries. The forecasted conditions are divided into four forecast periods, 12-, 24-, 36-, and 48-hours. Each chart depicts a "snapshot" of weather elements expected at the specified valid time.

These charts can be used to obtain an overview of the progression of surface weather features during the next 48 hours.

## 7. Describe a U.S. Low-Level Significant Weather Prog chart. (AC 00-45)

It is a "Day One" forecast of significant weather for the conterminous U.S. for the layer from surface to FL240 (400 mb). The chart is composed of four panels with two forecast periods, 12 hours and 24 hours, which are issued four times a day at 00Z, 06Z, 12Z, and 18Z. The two lower panels depict the 12- and 24-hour surface progs and the two upper panels depict the 12- and 24-hour significant weather progs. Covered are forecast positions and characteristics of pressure systems, fronts, and precipitation. Much insight on the "big weather picture" can be gained by evaluating the individual fields of pressure patterns, fronts, precipitation, weather flying categories, freezing levels, and turbulence displayed on the chart.

## 8. Describe a Mid-Level Significant Weather (SIGWX) chart. (AC 00-45)

This chart provides a forecast and an overview of significant enroute weather phenomena over a range of flight levels from 10,000 feet MSL to FL450, and associated surface weather features. It is a "snapshot" of weather expected at the specified valid time and depicts numerous weather elements that can be hazardous to aviation. The AWC issues the 24-hour Mid-Level Significant Weather chart 4 times daily.

## 9. What information may be obtained from the U.S. High-Level Significant Weather Prog charts? (AC 00-45)

The high-level significant weather prog is used to get an overview of selected flying weather conditions above 24,000 feet. Conditions routinely appearing on the chart are:

a. jet streams

b. cumulonimbus clouds

c. turbulence

d. tropopause heights

e. surface fronts

f. significant tropical storm complexes including tropical cyclones

g. squall lines

h. volcanic eruption sites

i. sandstorms and dust storms

### 10. What is a convective outlook chart? (AC 00-45)

The convective outlook chart depicts areas forecast to have the potential for severe (tornado, wind gusts 50 knots or greater, or hail 3/4 inch diameter size or greater) and non-severe (general) convection and specific severe weather threats during the following three days. The chart defines areas of slight risk (SLGT), moderate risk (MDT) or high risk (HIGH) of severe thunderstorms for a 24-hour period beginning at 1200 UTC. The Day 1 and Day 2 Convective Outlooks also depict areas of general thunderstorms (GEN TSTMS), while the Day 1, Day 2, and Day 3 Convective Outlooks may use SEE TEXT for areas where convection may approach or slightly exceed severe criteria.

### 11. What are constant pressure analysis charts? (AC 00-45)

Any surface of equal pressure in the atmosphere is a constant pressure surface. A constant pressure analysis chart is an upper air weather map where all information depicted is at the specified pressure of the chart. From these charts, a pilot can approximate the observed air temperature, wind, and temperature/dewpoint spread along a proposed route. They also depict highs, lows, troughs, and ridges aloft by the height contour patterns resembling isobars on a surface map. Twice daily, five computer-prepared constant pressure charts are issued from observed data:

| | |
|---|---|
| 850 mb | 5,000 ft |
| 700 mb | 10,000 ft |
| 500 mb | 18,000 ft |
| 300 mb | 30,000 ft |
| 200 mb | 39,000 ft |

**12. What significance do height contour lines have on a constant pressure chart?** (AC 00-45)

Heights of the specified pressure for each station are analyzed through the use of solid lines called contours to give a height pattern. The contours depict highs, lows, troughs, and ridges aloft in the same manner as isobars on the surface chart. Also, closely-spaced contours mean strong winds, as do closely-spaced isobars.

**13. What significance do isotherms have on a constant pressure chart?** (AC 00-45)

Isotherms (dashed lines) drawn at 5°C-intervals show horizontal temperature variations at chart altitude. By inspecting isotherms, you can determine if your flight will be toward colder or warmer air. Subfreezing temperatures and a temperature/dewpoint spread of 5°C or less suggest possible icing.

**14. What is the significance of the isotach lines on a constant pressure chart?** (AC 00-45)

Isotachs are lines of constant wind speed analyzed on the 300 and 200 mb charts; they separate higher wind speeds from lower wind speeds and are used to map wind speed variations over a surface. Isotachs are drawn at 20-knot intervals and begin at 10 knots. Isotach gradients identify the magnitude of wind speed variations. Strong gradients are closely spaced isotachs and identify large wind speed variations. Weak gradients are loosely spaced isotachs and identify small wind speed variations. Zones of very strong winds are highlighted by hatches.

# Additional Study Questions

1. Do the regulations require an operative pitot heater or alternate static source for IFR flight? (14 CFR 91.205)

2. What is the function of the "Kollsman" window on the altimeter? (FAA-H-8083-15)

3. What is the definition of a "standard-rate turn"? (FAA-H-8083-15)

4. Discuss the various types of weather reports a pilot would use to determine enroute weather. (AC 00-45)

5. Where can a pilot find information on the altitudes of cloud-layer tops? (AC 00-45)

6. The ATIS broadcast wind direction and speed are given in what values: magnetic or true north; knots or mph? (AIM 4-1-13)

7. If a thunderstorm forms along your route of flight, what distance should you maintain while attempting to fly around that thunderstorm? (AC 00-6A)

8. When considering potential alternate airports, must an airport have an instrument approach to be legal as an alternate? (14 CFR 91.169)

9. Not all airports can be used as alternate airports. Why? (FAA-H-8261-1)

# Departure

**2**

# A. Authority and Limitations of the Pilot

## 1. Discuss 14 CFR §91.3, "Responsibility and Authority of PIC." (14 CFR 91.3)

The pilot-in-command of an aircraft is directly responsible for, and is the final authority as to the operation of that aircraft.

## 2. What are the right-of-way rules pertaining to IFR flights? (14 CFR 91.113)

When weather conditions permit, regardless of whether an operation is under IFR or VFR, vigilance shall be maintained by each person operating an aircraft so as to see and avoid other aircraft.

## 3. What are the required reports for equipment malfunction under IFR in controlled airspace? (AIM 5-3-3)

You must report:

a. Any loss in controlled airspace of VOR, TACAN, ADF, or low-frequency navigation receiver capability.

b. GPS anomalies while using installed IFR-certified GPS/GNSS receivers.

c. Complete or partial loss of ILS receiver capability.

d. Impairment of air/ground communication capability.

e. Loss of any other equipment installed in the aircraft which may impair safety and/or the ability to operate under IFR.

# B. Departure Clearance

## 1. How can your IFR clearance be obtained? (AIM 5-1-8)

a. At airports with an ATC tower in operation, clearances may be received from either ground control or a specific clearance delivery frequency when available.

b. At airports without a tower or FSS on the field, or in an outlying area:

- Clearances may be received over the radio through a RCO (remote communication outlet) or, in some cases, over the telephone.

- In some areas, a clearance delivery frequency is available that is usable at different airports within a particular geographic area, for example, Class B airspace.

- If the above methods are not available, your clearance can be obtained from ARTCC once you are airborne, provided you remain VFR in Class E airspace.

The procedure may vary due to geographical features, weather conditions, and the complexity of the ATC system. To determine the most effective means of receiving an IFR clearance, pilots should ask the nearest FSS for the most appropriate means of obtaining their IFR clearance.

## 2. What does "cleared as filed" mean? (AIM 5-2-5)

ATC will issue an abbreviated IFR clearance based on the route of flight as filed in the IFR flight plan, provided the filed route can be approved with little or no revision.

## 3. Which clearance items are given in an abbreviated IFR clearance? (AIM 4-4-3 and 5-2-5)

**C** learance Limit (destination airport or fix)
**R** oute (initial heading)
**A** ltitude (initial altitude)
**F** requency (departure)
**T** ransponder (squawk code)

*Note:* ATC procedures now require the controller to state the DP name, the current number and the DP transition name after the phrase "Cleared to (destination) airport" and prior to the phrase, "then as filed," for ALL departure clearances when the DP or DP transition is to be flown.

### 4. What does "clearance void time" mean? (AIM 5-2-6)

When operating from an airport without a tower, a pilot may receive a clearance containing a provision that if the flight has not departed by a specific time, the clearance is void.

A pilot who does not depart prior to the clearance void time must advise ATC as soon as possible of his/her intentions. ATC will normally notify the pilot of the time allotted to notify ATC. This time cannot exceed 30 minutes.

### 5. What is the purpose of the term "hold for release" when included in an IFR clearance? (AIM 5-2-6)

ATC may issue "hold for release" instructions in a clearance to delay an aircraft's departure for traffic management reasons (weather, traffic volume, etc.). A pilot may not depart utilizing that IFR clearance until a release time or additional instructions are received from ATC.

## C. Departure Procedures

### 1. What minimums are necessary for IFR takeoff under 14 CFR Part 91? Under 121, 125, 129, or 135? (14 CFR 91.175)

For 14 CFR Part 91, none. For aircraft operated under 14 CFR Parts 121, 125, 129, or 135, if takeoff minimums are not prescribed under Part 97 for a particular airport, the following minimums apply to takeoffs under IFR for aircraft operating under those parts:

a.  For aircraft having two engines or less — 1 statute mile visibility.

b.  For aircraft having more than two engines — 1/2 statute mile visibility.

## 2. What is considered "good operating practice" in determining takeoff minimums for IFR flight?

If an instrument approach procedure has been prescribed for that airport, use the minimums for that approach for takeoff. If no approach procedure is available, basic VFR minimums are recommended (1,000 feet and 3 miles).

## 3. What are DPs and why are they necessary? (AIM 5-2-8)

Departure procedures are preplanned IFR procedures that provide obstruction clearance from the terminal area to the appropriate enroute structure. The primary reason they are established is to provide obstacle clearance protection. Also, at busier airports, they increase efficiency and reduce communication and departure delays. Pilots operating under Part 91 are strongly encouraged to file and fly a DP at night, during marginal VMC and IMC, when one is available.

## 4. What are the two types of DPs? (AIM 5-2-8)

a. ODPs (Obstacle Departure Procedures)—printed either textually or graphically, provide obstruction clearance via the least onerous route from the terminal area to the appropriate en route structure. ODPs are recommended for obstruction clearance and may be flown without ATC clearance unless an alternate departure procedure (SID or radar vector) has been specifically assigned by ATC.

b. SIDs (Standard Instrument Departures)—always printed graphically. Standard Instrument Departures are air traffic control (ATC) procedures printed for pilot/controller use in graphic form to provide obstruction clearance and a transition from the terminal area to the appropriate en route structure. SIDs are primarily designed for system enhancement and to reduce pilot/controller workload. ATC clearance must be received prior to flying a SID.

**5. What criteria are used to provide obstruction clearance during departure?** (AIM 5-2-8)

Unless specified otherwise, required obstacle clearance for all published departures is based on the pilot crossing the departure end of the runway (flying runway heading or reciprocal) at least 35 feet above the departure end of runway elevation, climbing to 400 feet above the departure end of runway elevation before making the initial turn, and maintaining a minimum climb gradient of 200 feet per nautical mile, unless required to level off by a crossing restriction. A greater climb gradient may be specified in the DP to clear obstacles or to achieve an ATC crossing restriction.

**6. Where are DPs located?** (AIM 5-2-8)

DPs will be listed by airport in "IFR Take-Off Minimums and Departure Procedures," Section C of the Terminal Procedures Publications (TPPs).

**7. Must you accept a SID if assigned one?** (AIM 5-2-8)

No. Pilots of civil aircraft operating from locations where SIDs are established may expect ATC clearances containing a SID. Use of a SID requires pilot possession of the textual description or graphic depiction of the approved current SID, as appropriate. RNAV SIDs must be retrievable by the procedure name from the aircraft database and conform to charted procedure. ATC must be immediately advised if the pilot does not possess the assigned SID, or the aircraft is not capable of flying the SID. Notification may be accomplished by filing "NO SID" in the remarks section of the filed flight plan or by the less desirable method of verbally advising ATC.

**8. How does a pilot determine if takeoff minimums are not standard and/or departure procedures are published for an airport?** (FAA-H-8261-1)

If an airport has non-standard takeoff minimums, a "triangle T" (or, "trouble T") symbol—that is, a black triangle with a T inside it—will be placed in the notes sections of the instrument procedure chart.

9. **When a DP specifies a climb gradient in excess of 200 feet per nautical mile, what significance should this have to the pilot?** (AIM 5-2-8)

If an aircraft may turn in any direction from a runway, and remain clear of obstacles, that runway passes what is called diverse departure criteria and no ODP will be published. A SID may be published if needed for air traffic control purposes. However, if an obstacle penetrates what is called the 40:1 slope obstacle identification surface, then the procedure designer chooses whether to:

   a. Establish a steeper than normal climb gradient; or

   b. Establish a steeper than normal climb gradient with an alternative that increases takeoff minima to allow the pilot to visually remain clear of the obstacle(s); or

   c. Design and publish a specific departure route; or

   d. A combination or all of the above.

10. **A climb gradient of 300 feet per nautical mile at a ground speed of 100 knots requires what rate of climb?** (Instrument Approach Procedures DP Chart)

Ground speed divided by 60 minutes times climb gradient = feet per minute; therefore,

$$\frac{100}{60} \times 300 = 500 \text{ feet per minute}$$

11. **What is the recommended climb rate procedure, when issued a climb to an assigned altitude by ATC?** (AIM 4-4-10)

When ATC has not used the term "At Pilot's Discretion" nor imposed any climb or descent restrictions, pilots should initiate climb or descent promptly on acknowledgement of the clearance. Descend or climb at an optimum rate consistent with the operating characteristics of the aircraft to 1,000 feet above or below the assigned altitude, and then attempt to descend or climb at a rate of between 500 and 1,500 fpm until the assigned altitude is reached.

# D. VOR Accuracy Checks

## 1. What are the different methods for checking the accuracy of VOR equipment? (14 CFR 91.171)

a.  A VOR Test Signal (VOT) check; ±4°

b.  A ground checkpoint; ±4°

c.  An airborne checkpoint; ±6°

d.  A dual VOR check; within 4° of each other

e.  Select a radial over a known ground point; ±6°

A repair station can use a radiated test signal, but only the technician performing the test can make an entry in the logbook.

## 2. What records must be kept concerning VOR checks? (14 CFR 91.171)

Each person making a VOR check shall enter the date, place and bearing error, and sign the aircraft log or other reliable record.

## 3. Where can a pilot find the location of airborne checkpoints, ground checkpoints and VOT testing stations? (AIM 1-1-4)

Locations of airborne checkpoints, ground checkpoints, and VOTs are published in the A/FD.

## 4. What procedure is used when checking VOR receiver accuracy with a VOT? (FAA-H-8083-15)

Tune in the VOT frequency of 108.0 MHz. With CDI centered, the OBS should read 0 degrees with TO/FROM indication showing FROM or the OBS should read 180 degrees with the TO/FROM indication showing TO.

*Remember:* "Cessna 182" — 180 TO for VOR accuracy checks using a VOT.

# E. Transponder

## 1. Where is altitude encoding transponder equipment required? (AIM 4-1-20)

In general, the regulations require aircraft to be equipped with Mode C transponders when operating:

a. At or above 10,000 feet MSL over the 48 contiguous states or the District of Columbia, excluding that airspace below 2,500 feet AGL;

b. Within 30 miles of a Class B airspace primary airport, below 10,000 feet MSL;

c. Within and above all Class C airspace, up to 10,000 feet MSL;

d. Within 10 miles of certain designated airports, excluding that airspace which is both outside the Class D surface area and below 1,200 feet AGL;

e. All aircraft flying into, within, or across the contiguous United States ADIZ.

## 2. What are the following transponder codes? (AIM 4-1-20, 6-2-2, 6-3-4, and 6-4-2)

| | |
|---|---|
| 1200 | VFR |
| 7700 | Emergency |
| 7600 | Communications Emergency |
| 7500 | Hijacking in progress |

## 3. Discuss transponder operation in the event of a two-way communications failure. (AIM 6-4-2)

If an aircraft with a coded radar beacon transponder experiences a loss of two-way radio capability, the pilot should adjust the transponder to reply on Mode A/3, Code 7600.

*Note:* The pilot should understand that the aircraft might not be in an area of radar coverage.

4. **Would an incorrect altimeter setting have an effect on the Mode C altitude information transmitted by your transponder?** (AIM 4-1-20)

No. While an incorrect altimeter setting has no effect on the Mode C altitude information transmitted by your transponder (transponders are preset at 29.92), it would cause you to fly at an actual altitude different from your assigned altitude.

When a controller indicates that an altitude readout is invalid, the pilot should initiate a check to verify that the aircraft altimeter is set.

# F. Airport Facilities

1. **Where can a pilot find information concerning facilities available for a particular airport?** (AIM 9-1-4)

In the Airport/Facility Directory; it contains information concerning services available, communication data, navigational facilities, special notices, etc. The A/FD is reissued in its entirety every 56 days.

2. **What do the following acronyms stand for?**
(AIM 2-1-1, 2-1-2, and 2-1-3)

ALS................................................ Approach Light System
VASI............................................... Visual Approach Slope Indicator
PAPI .............................................. Precision Approach Path Indicator
REIL .............................................. Runway End Identifier Lights

3. **What color are runway edge lights?** (AIM 2-1-4)

The runway edge lights are white—except on instrument runways, yellow replaces white on the last 2,000 feet or half the runway length, whichever is less, to form a caution zone for landings.

**4. What colors and color combinations are standard airport rotating beacons?** (AIM 2-1-8)

Lighted Land Airport ...................... White/Green
Lighted Water Airport ................... White/Yellow
Military Airport ............................ 2 White/Green

**5. What does the operation of a rotating beacon at an airport within Class D airspace during daylight hours mean?** (AIM 2-1-8)

In Class B, Class C, Class D, and Class E surface areas, operation of the airport beacon during the hours of daylight often indicates that the ground visibility is less than 3 miles and/or the ceiling is less than 1,000 feet. ATC clearance in accordance with 14 CFR Part 91 is required for landing, takeoff and flight in the traffic pattern. Pilots should not rely solely on the operation of the airport beacon to indicate if weather conditions are IFR or VFR. There is no regulatory requirement for daylight operation and it is the pilot's responsibility to comply with proper preflight planning as required by 14 CFR Part 91.

**6. Where would information concerning runway lengths, widths and weight bearing capacities be found?** (A/FD)

The Airport/Facility Directory has this information.

**7. What are runway touchdown zone markings?** (AIM 2-3-3)

Touchdown zone markings identify the touchdown zone for landing operations and are coded to provide distance information in 500-foot increments. These markings consist of groups of one, two, and three rectangular bars symmetrically arranged in pairs about the runway centerline. Normally, the standard glide slope angle of 3 degrees, if flown to the surface, will ensure touchdown within this zone.

## 8. What is the purpose of runway aiming point markings? (AIM 2-3-3)

The aiming point markings serve as a visual aiming point for a landing aircraft. These two rectangular markings consist of a broad white stripe, located on each side of the runway centerline, and approximately 1,000 feet from the landing threshold. The pilot can estimate a visual glide path that will intersect the marking ensuring a landing within the 3,000-foot touchdown zone.

## 9. How far down a runway does the touchdown zone extend? (P/CG)

The touchdown zone is the first 3,000 feet of the runway beginning at the threshold. The area is used for determination of Touchdown Zone Elevation in the development of straight-in landing minimums for instrument approaches.

## 10. What does the acronym "RWSL" stand for? (AIM 2-1-6)

Runway Status Light System—a fully automated system that provides runway status to pilots and surface vehicle operators to indicate clearly when it is unsafe to enter, cross, or takeoff from a runway. The system processes information from surveillance systems and illuminates Runway Entrance Lights (REL) and Takeoff Hold Lights (THL) in accordance with the motion of the detected traffic. The status lights have two states—ON: lights are illuminated red, and OFF: lights are not illuminated.

## 11. Does illumination of RWSL give a pilot permission to enter, cross, or takeoff from a runway? (AIM 2-1-6)

RWSL is an independent safety enhancement that does not substitute for an ATC clearance. Clearance to enter, cross, or takeoff from a runway must be issued by ATC. ATC personnel do not directly use, and may not be able to view, light fixture output in their operations even though ATC has limited control over the system.

# Additional Study Questions

1. What are pre-taxi clearance procedures? How do you determine if they are available? (AIM 5-2-1)

2. What responsibilities does a pilot have concerning readback of ATC clearances and instructions? (AIM 4-4-7)

3. Is an ATC clearance an authorization for a pilot to deviate from any rule, regulation or minimum altitude? (AIM 4-4-1)

4. ATC may issue a "release" time to an IFR flight. What significance does this have? (AIM 5-2-6)

5. What procedures should be used to determine that ADF equipment in the aircraft is functional? (FAA-H-8083-15)

6. What is the difference between a VFR Over-The-Top clearance and a VFR-On-Top clearance? (FAA-H-8083-15)

7. What are tower en route clearances? When would you request one? (AIM 4-1-19)

# En Route

**3**

# A. Enroute Limitations

## 1. Define the following. (P/CG)

MEA—Minimum Enroute Altitude; the lowest published altitude between radio fixes that ensures acceptable navigational signal coverage and meets obstacle clearance requirements.

MOCA—Minimum Obstruction Clearance Altitude; the lowest published altitude between radio fixes on VOR airways, off-airway routes, or route segments that meets obstacle clearance requirements, and that ensures acceptable navigational signal coverage only within 25 statute (22 nautical) miles of a VOR.

MCA—Minimum Crossing Altitude; the lowest altitude at certain fixes at which aircraft must cross when proceeding in the direction of a higher MEA.

MRA—Minimum Reception Altitude; the lowest altitude at which an intersection can be determined.

MAA—Maximum Authorized Altitude; the maximum usable altitude or flight level for an airspace structure or a route segment that ensures adequate reception of navigation aid signals.

OROCA—Off-Route Obstruction Clearance Altitude; this provides obstruction clearance with a 1,000-foot buffer in non-mountainous terrain areas and a 2,000-foot buffer in designated mountainous areas within the United States. This altitude might not provide signal coverage from ground-based navigational aids, Air Traffic Control radar, or communications coverage.

## 2. If no applicable minimum altitude is prescribed (no MEA or MOCA), what minimum altitudes apply for IFR operations? (14 CFR 91.177 and Part 95)

Minimum altitudes are:

a. Mountainous terrain—at least 2,000 feet above the highest obstacle within a horizontal distance of 4 NM from the course to be flown.

b. Other than mountainous terrain—at least 1,000 feet above the highest obstacle within a horizontal distance of 4 NM from the course to be flown.

3. **What cruising altitudes shall be maintained while operating under IFR in controlled airspace (Class A, B, C, D, or E)? In uncontrolled airspace (Class G)?** (14 CFR 91.179)

IFR flights within controlled airspace (Class A, B, C, D, or E) shall maintain the altitude or flight level assigned by ATC. In uncontrolled airspace (Class G), altitude is selected based on the magnetic course flown:

Below 18,000 feet MSL:

0 to 179°......................................... odd thousand MSL
180 to 359°..................................... even thousand MSL

18,000 feet up to but not including 29,000 feet MSL:

0 to 179°......................................... odd flight levels
180 to 359°..................................... even flight levels

4. **What procedures are applicable concerning courses to be flown when operating IFR?** (14 CFR 91.181)

Unless otherwise authorized by ATC, no one may operate an aircraft within controlled airspace under IFR except on an air traffic services (ATS) route, along the centerline of that airway, or on any other route along the direct course between the navigational aids or fixes defining that route. However, this does not prohibit maneuvering the aircraft to pass well clear of other air traffic, or maneuvering in VFR conditions to clear the intended flight path both before and during climb or descent.

5. **On a direct flight not flown on radials or courses of established airways or routes, what points serve as compulsory reporting points?** (AIM 5-3-2)

Along direct routes, reports are required of all IFR flights over each point used to define the route of flight.

### 6. What are "unpublished" RNAV routes? (AIM 5-3-4)

Unpublished RNAV routes are direct routes based on area navigation capability, between waypoints defined in terms of latitude/
longitude coordinates, degree-distance fixes, or offsets from established routes/airways at a specified distance and direction. Radar
monitoring by ATC is required on all unpublished RNAV routes.

## B. Enroute Procedures

### 1. What reports should be made to ATC at all times without a specific request? (AIM 5-3-3)

The pilot must report:

a. When vacating any previously assigned altitude or flight level
   for a newly assigned altitude or flight level.

b. When an altitude change will be made if operating on a clearance specifying VFR-On-Top.

c. When unable to climb/descend at a rate of at least 500 feet
   per minute.

d. When approach has been missed (request clearance for specific
   action; i.e., to alternate airport, another approach, etc.).

e. Change in the average true speed (at cruising altitude) when it
   varies by 5 percent or 10 knots (whichever is greater) from that
   filed in the flight plan.

f. The time and altitude or flight level upon reaching a holding fix
   or point that the pilot is cleared to.

g. When leaving any assigned holding fix or point.

h. Any loss, in controlled airspace, of VOR, TACAN, ADF,
   low-frequency navigation receiver capability, GPS anomalies
   while using installed IFR-certified GPS/GNSS receivers, complete or partial loss of ILS receiver capability or impairment of
   air/ground communications capability.

i. Any information relating to the safety of flight.

j. Upon encountering weather or hazardous conditions
   not forecast.

**2. What reporting requirements are required by ATC when not in radar contact?** (AIM 5-3-3)

a. When leaving final approach fix inbound on the final (nonprecision) approach, or when leaving the outer marker (or fix used in lieu of the outer marker) inbound on final (precision) approach.

b. A corrected estimate at anytime it becomes apparent that an estimate as previously submitted is in error in excess of 3 minutes.

**3. What items of information should be included in every position report?** (AIM 5-3-2)

a. Identification

b. Position

c. Time

d. Altitude or flight level

e. Type of flight plan (not required in IFR position reports made directly to ARTCCs or approach control)

f. ETA and name of next reporting point

g. The name only of the next succeeding reporting point along the route of flight, and

h. Pertinent remarks

**4. Are you required to report unforecast weather encountered en route?** (AIM 5-3-3)

Yes; pilots encountering weather conditions which have not been forecast, or hazardous conditions which have been forecast, are expected to forward a report of such weather to ATC.

**5. Explain the terms "maintain" and "cruise" as they pertain to an IFR altitude assignment.** (AIM 4-4-3)

*Maintain*—Self-explanatory: maintain last altitude assigned.

*Cruise*—Used instead of "maintain" to assign a block of airspace to a pilot, from minimum IFR altitude up to and including the altitude specified in the cruise clearance. The pilot may level off at any intermediate altitude, and climb/descent may be made at the discretion of the pilot. However, once the pilot starts a descent, and *verbally* reports leaving an altitude in the block, he may not return to that altitude without additional ATC clearance.

**6. Can a cruise clearance authorize you to execute an approach at the destination airport?** (FAA-H-8261-1)

Yes. ATC may issue a cruise clearance that authorizes you to execute an approach upon arrival at the destination airport. ATC will not issue further clearance for approach and landing. When operating in uncontrolled airspace on a cruise clearance, you are responsible for determining the minimum IFR altitude. In addition, descent and landing at an airport in uncontrolled airspace are governed by the applicable visual flight rules and/or operations specifications, i.e. 14 CFR §91.126, 91.155, 91.175, 91.179, etc.

**7. Why would a pilot request a VFR-On-Top clearance?** (AIM 4-4-8)

A pilot on an IFR flight plan operating in VFR weather conditions, may request VFR-On-Top in lieu of an assigned altitude. For reasons such as turbulence, more favorable winds aloft, etc., the pilot has the flexibility to select an altitude or flight level of his/her choice (subject to any ATC restrictions). Pilots desiring to climb through a cloud, haze, smoke, or other meteorological formation and then either cancel their IFR flight plan or operate VFR-On-Top may request a climb to VFR-On-Top.

**8. Is a VFR-On-Top clearance a VFR clearance or an IFR clearance?** (AIM 4-4-8)

A VFR-On-Top clearance is an IFR clearance.

**9. Which airspace prohibits VFR-On-Top clearances?** (AIM 4-4-8)

Class A airspace.

## 10. What operational procedures must pilots on IFR flight plans adhere to when operating VFR-On-Top? (AIM 4-4-8)

They must:

a. Fly at the appropriate VFR altitude

b. Comply with the VFR visibility and distance from cloud criteria

c. Comply with instrument flight rules that are applicable to this flight; i.e., minimum IFR altitudes, position reporting, radio communications, course to be flown, adherence to ATC clearance, etc.

## 11. What is a "clearance limit" and when is it received? (AIM 4-4-3)

A traffic clearance issued prior to departure will normally authorize flight to the airport of intended landing. Under certain conditions, at some locations, a short-range clearance procedure is used, whereby a clearance is issued to a fix within or just outside of the terminal area, and pilots are advised of the frequency on which they will receive the long-range clearance direct from the center controller.

## 12. What information will ATC provide when they request a hold at a fix where the holding pattern is not charted? (AIM 5-3-7)

An ATC clearance requiring an aircraft to hold at a fix where the pattern is not charted will include the following information:

a. Direction of holding from the fix, in reference to the eight cardinal compass points (i.e. N, NE, E, SE, etc.).

b. Holding fix (the fix may be omitted if included at the beginning of the transmission as the clearance limit).

c. Radial, course, bearing, airway or route on which the aircraft is to hold.

d. Leg length in miles if DME or RNAV is to be used (leg length will be specified in minutes on pilot request or if the controller considers it necessary).

e. Direction of turns, if holding pattern is nonstandard (left turns), the pilot requests direction of turns, or the controller considers it necessary to state direction of turns.

f. Time to expect further clearance and any pertinent additional delay information.

## 13. What are the maximum airspeeds permitted for aircraft while holding? (AIM 5-3-7)

MHA – 6,000 ft.............................. 200 KIAS
6,001 – 14,000 ft............................. 230 KIAS
14,001 – and above ......................... 265 KIAS

*Note:* Holding patterns may be restricted to a maximum speed. Holding patterns from 6,001 to 14,000 feet may be restricted to a maximum airspeed of 210 KIAS. These nonstandard patterns will be depicted by an icon.

## 14. What is a nonstandard versus a standard holding pattern? (AIM 5-3-7)

In a standard pattern, all turns are to the right. In a nonstandard pattern, all turns are to the left.

## 15. Describe the procedure for crosswind correction in a holding pattern. (AIM 5-3-7)

Compensate for wind effect primarily by drift correction on the inbound and outbound legs. When outbound, triple the inbound drift correction to avoid major turning adjustments.

## 16. What action is appropriate when approaching a holding fix at an airspeed in excess of maximum holding speed? (AIM 5-3-7)

Start a speed reduction when 3 minutes or less from the fix. Speed may be reduced earlier, but ATC must be advised of the change.

**17. Why is it important for the pilot to receive an EFC time with initial holding instructions?** (AIM 5-3-7)

If you lose two-way radio communication, the EFC allows you to depart the holding fix at a definite time. Plan the last lap of your holding pattern to leave the fix as close as possible to the exact time.

**18. Describe the different recommended entry methods for holding.** (AIM 5-3-7)

The three types of entry are:

a. Parallel
b. Teardrop
c. Direct

**19. What is the leg length for a standard holding pattern?** (AIM 5-3-7)

The standard leg length is:

a. 1 minute inbound at or below 14,000 feet MSL, and

b. 1½ minutes inbound above 14,000 feet MSL.

**20. If assigned a DME/GPS hold, what procedures should be used?** (AIM 5-3-7)

Distance Measuring Equipment (DME)/GPS Along-Track Distance (ATD) holding is subject to the same entry and holding procedures except that distances (nautical miles) are used in lieu of time values. The outbound course of the DME/GPS holding pattern is called the outbound leg of the pattern. The controller or the instrument approach procedure chart will specify the length of the outbound leg. The end of the outbound leg is determined by the DME or ATD readout.

**21. When does the timing for the outbound leg in a holding pattern begin?** (AIM 5-3-7)

Outbound leg timing begins over/abeam the fix, whichever occurs later. If the abeam position cannot be determined, start timing when turn to outbound is completed.

## C. Oxygen Requirements

### 1. What regulations apply concerning supplemental oxygen? (14 CFR 91.211)

a. At cabin pressure altitudes above 12,500 MSL up to and including 14,000 MSL, the minimum flight crew must use oxygen after 30 minutes.

b. Above 14,000 MSL up to and including 15,000 MSL, the minimum flight crew must continuously use oxygen.

c. Above 15,000 MSL, each passenger must be provided with supplemental oxygen and the minimum flight crew must continuously use oxygen.

## D. Emergencies

### 1. When may the pilot-in-command of an aircraft deviate from an ATC clearance? (14 CFR 91.123)

Except in an emergency, no person may, in an area in which air traffic control is exercised, operate an aircraft contrary to an ATC instruction.

### 2. If an emergency action requires deviation from 14 CFR Part 91, must a pilot submit a written report, and if so, to whom? (14 CFR 91.123)

Each pilot-in-command who is given priority by ATC in an emergency shall, if requested by ATC, submit a detailed report of that emergency within 48 hours to the manager of that ATC facility.

3. **Concerning two-way radio communications failure in VFR and IFR conditions, what is the procedure for altitude, route, leaving holding fix, descent for approach, and approach selection?** (14 CFR 91.185)

*In VFR conditions:* If the failure occurs in VFR, or if VFR is encountered after the failure, each pilot shall continue the flight under VFR and land as soon as practicable.

*In IFR conditions:* If the failure occurs in IFR conditions, or if VFR conditions are not within range, each pilot shall continue the flight according to the following:

a. Route:

**A** ssigned.......... by route assigned in last ATC clearance

**V** ectored.......... go direct from point of radio failure to fix, route, airway in vector clearance

**E** xpected......... by route that ATC has advised may be expected

**F** iled................ by the route filed in flight plan

b. Altitude (highest of following altitudes for the route segment being flown):

**M** inimum......... minimum altitude for IFR operations

**E** xpected......... altitude/flight level ATC has advised to expect in a further clearance

**A** ssigned.......... altitude/flight level assigned in the last ATC clearance

c. Leave clearance limit:

• When the clearance limit is a fix from which the approach begins, commence descent or descent and approach as close as possible to the expect-further-clearance time if one has been received; or if one has not been received, as close as possible to the estimated time of arrival as calculated from the filed or amended (with ATC) estimated time en route.

• If the clearance limit is not a fix from which the approach begins, leave the clearance limit at the expect-further-clearance time if one has been received; or if none has been received, upon arrival over the clearance limit, and proceed to a fix from which an approach begins and commence descent or decent and approach as close as possible to the estimated time of arrival as calculated from the filed or amended (with ATC) estimated time en route.

4. **Assuming two-way communications failure, discuss the recommended procedure to follow concerning altitudes to be flown for the following trip:**

   **The MEA between A and B is 5,000 feet; the MEA between B and C is 5,000 feet; the MEA between C and D is 11,000 feet; and the MEA between D and E is 7,000 feet. You have been cleared via A, B, C, D, to E. While flying between A and B, your assigned altitude was 6,000 feet and you were told to expect a clearance to 8,000 feet at B. Prior to receiving the higher altitude assignment, you experience two-way communication failure.** (AIM 6-4-1)

   The correct procedure would be as follows:

   a. Maintain 6,000 feet to B, then climb to 8,000 feet (the altitude you were advised to expect).

   b. Continue to maintain 8,000 feet, then climb to 11,000 feet at C, or prior to C if necessary to comply with an MCA at C.

   c. Upon reaching D, you would descend to 8,000 feet (even though the MEA was 7,000 feet), as 8,000 feet was the highest of the altitude situations stated in the rule.

5. **What procedure would you use if all communication and navigation equipment failed (complete electrical system failure)?**

   a. First, determine you have complete loss. Determine the cause (check circuit breakers, alternator, ammeter, etc.).

   b. Review the preflight weather briefing for the nearest VFR; determine heading and altitude and proceed to VFR conditions, using VFR altitudes.

   c. If VFR conditions are not within range of the aircraft, get off the airway and determine the heading to an unpopulated area relatively free of obstructions (terrain or man-made; i.e., rural areas, large lakes, ocean, etc.).

   d. Establish a descent on a specific heading to VFR conditions; proceed VFR to the nearest airport.

6. **What does Single-Pilot Resource Management refer to?**
   (FAA-S-8081-4)

   Single-Pilot Resource Management (SRM) refers to the effective
   use of *all* available resources: human resources, hardware, and
   information. Human resources include all other groups routinely
   working with the pilot who are involved in decisions that are
   required to operate a flight safely. These groups include, but are
   not limited to: dispatchers, weather briefers, maintenance personnel, and air traffic controllers. SRM is similar to Crew Resource
   Management (CRM) procedures.

# E. Radio Orientation

1. **What angular deviation from a VOR course is
   represented by half-scale deflection of the CDI?**
   (FAA-H-8083-15)

   Full scale deflection = 10°; therefore, half-scale deflection = 5°

2. **What is reverse sensing?** (FAA-H-8083-15)

   Reverse sensing is when the VOR needle indicates the reverse of
   normal operation. This occurs when the aircraft is headed toward
   the station with a FROM indication or when the aircraft is headed
   away from the station with a TO indication. Also, unless the aircraft has reverse sensing capability and it is in use, when flying
   inbound on the back course or outbound on the front course of an
   ILS, reverse sensing will occur.

3. **What is the procedure for determining an intercept angle
   when intercepting a VOR radial?** (FAA-H-8083-15)

   a. Turn to a heading to parallel the desired course, in the same
      direction as the course to be flown.

   b. Determine the difference between the radial to be intercepted
      and the radial on which you are located.

   c. Double the difference to determine the interception angle,
      which will not be less than 20° nor greater than 90°.

   d. Rotate the OBS to the desired radial or inbound course.

   e. Turn to the interception heading.

   f.  Hold this heading constant until the CDI centers, which indi-
       cates the aircraft is on course. (With practice in judging the
       varying rates of closure with the course centerline, you learn to
       lead the turn to prevent overshooting the course.)

   g.  Turn to the MH corresponding to the selected course, and fol-
       low tracking procedures inbound or outbound.

*Note:* Steps a. through c. may be omitted if you turn directly to
intercept the course without initially turning to parallel the desired
course.

### 4. What degree of accuracy can be expected in VOR navigation? (AIM 1-1-3)

VOR navigation is accurate to ±1°.

### 5. How do you find an ADF relative bearing? (FAA-H-8083-15)

A relative bearing is the angular relationship between the aircraft
heading and the station, measured clockwise from the nose. The
bearing is read directly on the ADF dial, measured clockwise
from zero.

### 6. How do you find an ADF magnetic bearing? (FAA-H-8083-15)

A magnetic bearing is the direction of an imaginary line from the
aircraft to the station or the station to the aircraft referenced to
magnetic north. To determine, use this formula:

MH + RB = MB

(Magnetic heading + relative bearing = magnetic bearing)

If the sum is more than 360, subtract 360 to get the magnetic bearing to the station. The reciprocal of this number is the magnetic
bearing from the station.

### 7. What is ADF homing? (FAA-H-8083-15)

ADF homing is flying the aircraft on any heading required to keep
the ADF needle on zero until the station is reached.

**8. What is ADF tracking?** (FAA-H-8083-15)

ADF tracking is a procedure used to fly a straight geographic flight path inbound to or from an NDB. A heading is established that will maintain the desired track, compensating for wind drift.

**9. You are tracking inbound to an NDB, your heading equals your course and the ADF needle is now pointing 10 degrees to the left. What procedure will you use for wind drift correction?** (FAA-H-8083-15)

Turn 20° left. When the needle is deflected 20° (deflection = interception angle), track has been intercepted. The aircraft is on track as long as the RB remains the same number of degrees as the wind correction angle (WCA). Lead the interception to avoid over-shooting the track. Turn 10° toward the inbound course. You are now inbound with a 10° left correction angle.

# F. Unusual Flight Conditions

**1. If a thunderstorm is inadvertently encountered, what flight instrument and what procedure should be used to maintain control of the aircraft?** (AC 00-6A, Ch. 11)

*Attitude Indicator*—establish power for the recommended maneuvering speed and attempt to maintain a constant *attitude* only. Do not attempt to maintain a constant *altitude*.

**2. What are the conditions needed for major structural icing to form?** (AC 00-6A, Ch. 10)

Two conditions are necessary for structural icing in flight:

a. The aircraft must be flying through visible water such as rain or cloud droplets, and

b. Temperature at the point where the moisture strikes the aircraft must be 0°C or colder. Aerodynamics cooling can lower temperature of an airfoil to 0°C even though the ambient temperature is a few degrees warmer.

3. **What action is recommended if you inadvertently encounter icing conditions?** (FAA-H-8083-15)

   a. Move to an altitude with significantly colder temperatures;

   b. Move to an altitude with temperatures that are above freezing;

   c. Fly to an area clear of visible moisture; or

   d. Change heading and fly to an area of known non-icing conditions.

4. **Which type of precipitation will produce the most hazardous icing conditions?** (AC 00-6A, Ch. 10)

   Freezing rain produces the most hazardous icing conditions.

5. **If icing is inadvertently encountered, how would your landing approach procedure be different?** (AC 00-6A, Ch. 10)

   The following guidelines may be used when flying an airplane which has accumulated ice:

   a. Maintain more power during the approach.

   b. Maintain a higher airspeed.

   c. Expect a higher stall speed.

   d. Expect a longer landing roll.

   e. A "no flaps" approach is recommended.

   f. Maintain a consistently higher altitude than normal.

   g. Avoid a missed approach (get it right the first time).

# G. Radio Navigation

### 1. Within what frequency range do VORs operate? (AIM 1-1-3)

VORs operate within the 108.0 to 117.95 MHz VHF band.

### 2. What are the normal usable distances for the various classes of VOR stations? (AIM 1-1-8)

H-VORs and L-VORs have a normal usable distance of 40 nautical miles below 18,000 feet. T-VORs are short-range facilities which have a power output of approximately 50 watts and a usable distance of 25 nautical miles at 12,000 feet and below. T-VORs are used primarily for instrument approaches in terminal areas, on or adjacent to airports.

| | | | |
|---|---|---|---|
| Terminal | = | 1,000 to 12,000 AGL | 25 NM |
| Low-altitude | = | 1,000 to 18,000 AGL | 40 NM |
| High-altitude | = | 1,000 to 14,500 AGL | 40 NM |
| High-altitude | = | 14,500 to 18,000 AGL | 100 NM |
| High-altitude | = | 18,000 to 45,000 AGL | 130 NM |
| High-altitude | = | 45,000 to 60,000 AGL | 100 NM |

### 3. What is the meaning of a single coded identification received only once every 30 seconds from a VORTAC station? (AIM 1-1-7 and 1-1-12)

The DME component is operative; the VOR component is inoperative. It is important to recognize which identifier is retained for the operative facility. A single coded identifier with a repeat interval every 30 seconds indicates DME is operative. If no identification is received, the facility has been taken off the air for tune-up or repair, even though intermittent or constant signals are received.

### 4. Will all VOR stations have capability for providing distance information to aircraft equipped with DME? (AIM 1-1-7)

No, aircraft receiving equipment ensures reception of azimuth and distance information from a common source only when designated as VOR/DME, VORTAC, ILS/DME, and LOC/DME stations.

5. **For IFR operations off established airways, the "Route of Flight" portion of an IFR flight plan should list VOR navigational aids which are no further than what distance from each other?** (AIM 5-1-8)

Below 18,000 feet MSL, use aids not more than 80 NM apart.

Between 14,500 feet MSL and 17,999 feet MSL in the conterminous U.S., H (high altitude service volume) facilities not more than 200 NM apart may be used.

6. **Within what frequency range do NDBs normally operate?** (AIM 1-1-2)

NDBs operate within the low- to medium-frequency band—190 to 535 kHz.

7. **When a radio beacon is used in conjunction with an ILS marker beacon, what is it called?** (AIM 1-1-2)

It is called a compass locator.

8. **There are four types of NDB facilities in use. What are they and what are their effective ranges?** (AIM 1-1-8)

HH facilities: 2,000 watts .............................. 75 NM
H facilities: 50 to 1,999 watts ........................ 50 NM
MH facilities: less than 50 watts .................... 25 NM
ILS compass locator: less than 25 watts ......... 15 NM

9. **What limitations apply when using an NDB for navigation?** (AIM 1-1-2)

Radio beacons are subject to disturbances that may result in erroneous bearing information. Disturbances result from factors such as lightning, precipitation static, etc. At night, radio beacons are vulnerable to interference from distant stations.

10. **What operational procedure should be used when navigation or approaches are conducted using an NDB?** (AIM 1-1-2)

Since ADF receivers do not incorporate signal flags to warn a pilot when erroneous bearing information is being displayed, the pilot should continuously monitor the NDBs coded identification.

## 11. What is an HSI? (FAA-H-8083-15)

The horizontal situation indicator is a combination of two instruments, a vertical heading indicator and a VOR/ILS indicator. The aircraft heading is displayed under the upper lubber line. A course indicating arrow shows the course selected (head) and the reciprocal (tail). The course deviation bar operates with a VOR/LOC navigation receiver to indicate left or right deviations for the course selected. The fixed aircraft symbol and course deviation bar display the aircraft relative to the selected course as though you were above the aircraft looking down. The triangular-shaped pointer is the TO-FROM indicator. The glide slope deviation pointer indicates the relation of the aircraft to the glide slope.

## 12. What is an RMI? (FAA-H-8083-15)

The radio magnetic indicator consists of a rotating compass card, a double-barred bearing indicator, and a single-barred bearing indicator. The compass card, actuated by the compass system, rotates as the aircraft turns. The bearing pointers display ADF or VOR magnetic bearings to the selected station. In most installations, the double-barred bearing indicator gives the magnetic bearing to the VOR or VORTAC and the single-barred indicator is an ADF needle which gives the magnetic bearing to the selected low-frequency facility.

The tail of the double-barred indicator tells you the radial you are on, and the tail of the single-barred indicator tells you your magnetic bearing from a low-frequency station.

## 13. What is DME? (AIM 1-1-7)

DME stands for *Distance Measuring Equipment*. Aircraft equipped with DME are provided with distance and ground speed information when receiving a VORTAC or TACAN facility. In the operation of DME, paired pulses at a specific spacing are sent out from the aircraft and are received at the ground station. The ground station then transmits paired pulses back to the aircraft at the same pulse spacing but on a different frequency. The time required for the round trip of this signal exchange is measured in the airborne

DME unit and is translated into distance and ground speed. Reliable signals may be received at distances up to 199 NM at line-of-sight altitude. DME operates on frequencies in the UHF spectrum between 960 MHz to 1215 MHz. Distance information is slant-range distance, not horizontal.

## 14. When is DME equipment required? (14 CFR 91.205)

If VOR navigational equipment is required for flight at and above FL240, the aircraft must be equipped with approved DME or a suitable RNAV system. If the DME or RNAV system should fail at and above FL240, the pilot-in-command shall notify ATC immediately, and then may continue operations to the next airport of intended landing where repairs or equipment replacement can be done.

## 15. As a rule of thumb, to minimize DME slant range error, how far from the facility should you be to consider the reading accurate? (FAA-H-8083-15)

Slant range error will be at a minimum if the aircraft is one or more miles from the facility for each 1,000 feet of altitude above the facility.

## 16. What is RNAV? (P/CG)

Area Navigation (RNAV) provides enhanced navigational capability to the pilot. RNAV equipment can compute the airplane position, actual track and ground speed and then provide meaningful information relative to a route of flight selected by the pilot. Typical equipment will provide the pilot with distance, time, bearing and crosstrack error relative to the selected "TO" or "active" waypoint and the selected route. Several distinctly different navigational systems with different navigational performance characteristics are capable of providing area navigational functions. Present day RNAV includes INS, LORAN, VOR/DME, and GPS systems.

## 17. What is LORAN? (P/CG)

LORAN is an abbreviation for Long Range Navigation. It is an electronic navigation system by which hyperbolic lines of position are determined by measuring the difference in the time of reception of synchronized pulse signals from two fixed transmitters. A LORAN receiver is basically an onboard computer capable of determining an aircraft's position based on the measurement of time-difference receipt of these different signals. LORAN receivers also have computer memory capable of storing information and useful programs such as airport locations, navigational aids, etc., and programs such as estimated time to station, ground speed, true airspeed, bearing to nearest airport, etc.

## 18. Give a brief description of GPS. (AIM 1-1-19)

Global Positioning System (GPS) is a satellite-based radio navigation system that broadcasts a signal used by receivers to determine precise position anywhere in the world. The receiver tracks multiple satellites and determines a pseudo-range measurement that is then used to determine the user location.

## 19. What are the three functional elements of GPS?
(FAA-H-8083-15)

a. The *space* element consists of 24 Navstar satellites (called a "constellation"). The satellites are in six orbital planes (with four in each plane) at about 11,000 miles above the earth. At least five satellites are in view at all times.

b. The *control* element consists of a network of ground-based GPS monitoring and control stations that ensure the accuracy of satellite positions and their clocks. In its present form, it has five monitoring stations, three ground antennas, and a master control station.

c. The *user* element consists of antennas and receiver–processors onboard the aircraft that provide positioning, velocity, and precise timing to the user.

**20. Is an alternate means of navigation appropriate to the route of flight required if using GPS navigation equipment under IFR?** (AIM 1-1-19)

Yes. Aircraft using GPS navigation equipment under IFR must be equipped with an approved and operational alternate means of navigation appropriate to the flight. Active monitoring of alternative navigation equipment is not required if the GPS receiver uses RAIM for integrity monitoring. Active monitoring of an alternate means of navigation is required when the RAIM capability of the GPS equipment is lost.

*Note:* Aircraft equipped with a WAAS receiver may use WAAS as a primary means of navigation. No additional equipment is required.

**21. What is the purpose of "RAIM"?** (AIM 1-1-19)

The GPS receiver verifies the integrity (usability) of the signals received from the GPS constellation through receiver autonomous integrity monitoring (RAIM) to determine if a satellite is providing corrupted information. At least one satellite, in addition to those required for navigation, must be in view for the receiver to perform the RAIM function; thus, RAIM needs a minimum of 5 satellites in view, or 4 satellites and a barometric altimeter (baro-aiding) to detect an integrity anomaly.

**22. If RAIM capability is lost while conducting IFR enroute or approach operations, can you continue flight using GPS information?** (AIM 1-1-19)

No. Without RAIM capability, the GPS may no longer be providing the required accuracy. The pilot should select another type of navigation system until RAIM is restored.

## 23. Where can a pilot obtain RAIM availability information? (AIM 1-1-19)

Civilian pilots may obtain GPS RAIM availability information for nonprecision approach procedures by specifically requesting GPS aeronautical information from an Automated Flight Service Station during preflight briefings. FAA briefers will provide RAIM information for a period of 1 hour before to 1 hour after the ETA, unless a specific time frame is requested by the pilot.

## 24. Can handheld GPS receivers and GPS systems certified for VFR operations be used for IFR operations? (AIM 1-1-19)

No, for the following reasons:

a. RAIM capability—VFR GPS receivers and all handheld units have no RAIM alerting capability. Loss of the required number of satellites in view, or the detection of a position error, cannot be displayed to the pilot by such receivers.

b. Database currency—In many receivers, an updatable database is used for navigation fixes, airports, and instrument procedures. These databases must be maintained to the current update for IFR operation, but no such requirement exists for VFR use.

c. Antenna location—In many VFR installations of GPS receivers, antenna location is more a matter of convenience than performance. In IFR installations, care is exercised to ensure that an adequate clear view is provided for the antenna to see satellites. If an alternate location is used, some portion of the aircraft may block the view of the antenna, causing a greater opportunity to lose navigation.

*Note:* VFR and handheld GPS systems are not authorized for IFR navigation, instrument approaches, or as a principal instrument flight reference. During IFR operations they may be considered only as an aid to situational awareness.

# H. Airway Route System

### 1. What are the designated altitudes for the airways in the VOR and L/MF Airway System? (AIM 5-3-4)

The VOR and L/MF Airway System consists of airways designated from 1,200 feet above the surface (or in some instances higher) up to but not including 18,000 feet MSL. These airways are depicted on Enroute Low Altitude Charts.

### 2. What are the lateral limits of low altitude federal airways? (FAA-H-8083-15)

Each federal airway includes the airspace within parallel boundary lines 4 NM each side of the centerline.

### 3. How are federal airways depicted on Enroute Low Altitude Charts? (AIM 5-3-4)

Except in Alaska and coastal North Carolina, the VOR airways are predicated solely on VOR or VORTAC navigation aids; they are depicted in blue on aeronautical charts (black on Enroute Low Altitude Charts), and are identified by a "V" (Victor) followed by an airway number. A segment of an airway which is common to two or more routes carries the numbers of all the airways which coincide for that segment.

### 4. What is a "changeover point"? (AIM 5-3-6)

It is a point along the route or airway segment between two adjacent navigational facilities or waypoints where changeover in navigational guidance should occur.

### 5. What is a mileage breakdown point? (FAA-H-8083-15)

Occasionally an "x" will appear at a separated segment of an airway that is not an intersection. The "x" is a mileage breakdown or computer navigation fix and indicates a course change.

## 6. What is a "waypoint"? (P/CG)

It is a predetermined geographical position used for route/instrument approach definition, progress reports, published VFR routes, visual reporting points or points for transitioning and/or circumnavigating controlled and/or special use airspace. A waypoint is defined relative to a VORTAC station or in terms of latitude/longitude coordinates.

## 7. What are the two types of waypoints found on charts? (FAA-H-8261-1)

A fly-by waypoint typically is used in a position at which a change in the course of procedure occurs. Charts represent them with four-pointed stars. Fly-by waypoints are designed to allow you to anticipate and begin your turn prior to reaching the waypoint, thus providing smoother transitions. Fly-over waypoints are depicted as a four-pointed star enclosed in a circle. This type of waypoint is used to denote a missed approach point, a missed approach holding point, or other specific points in space that must be flown over.

## 8. Are the courses depicted on an Enroute Low Altitude Chart magnetic or true courses? (FAA-H-8083-15)

They are magnetic courses.

## 9. Describe the climb procedure when approaching a fix beyond which a higher MEA exists. (14 CFR 91.177)

A pilot may begin a climb to the new MEA at the fix.

## 10. Describe the climb procedure when approaching a fix at which a MCA exists. (FAA-H-8083-15)

A pilot should initiate a climb so the MCA is reached by the time the intersection is crossed. An MCA will be charted when a higher MEA route segment is approached. The MCA is usually indicated when you are approaching steeply rising terrain, and obstacle clearance and/or signal reception is compromised.

## 11. VHF/UHF and LF/MF route data will be depicted in what specific colors on Enroute Low Altitude Charts? (Enroute Low Altitude Chart Legend)

Airways based on VOR or VORTAC navaids are depicted in black and identified by a "V"(Victor) followed by the route number (e.g. "V12"). In Alaska, some segments of low-altitude airways are based on LF/MF navaids and are charted in brown instead of black.

## 12. What are "T" and "Q" routes? (AIM 5-3-4)

Published RNAV routes that can be flight-planned for use by aircraft with RNAV capability. They are depicted in blue on aeronautical charts and are identified by the letter T or Q, followed by the airway number (e.g., T-205, Q-13). They provide more direct routing for IFR aircraft and enhance system safety and efficiency.

*T-routes* — depicted on Enroute Low Altitude Charts; available for use by RNAV equipped aircraft from 1,200 feet above the surface (or in some instances higher) up to but not including 18,000 feet MSL.

*Q-routes* — depicted on Enroute High Altitude Charts; available for use by RNAV equipped aircraft between 18,000 feet MSL and FL450 inclusive.

## 13. For the following terms, identify the symbols which correspond to them on Enroute Low Altitude Charts.

*(These symbols might not all be on your Enroute Low Altitude Chart.)*

VOR /DME ............................................................................. ⬡

TACAN ................................................................................. ▽

VOR ..................................................................................... ⬡

VORTAC ............................................................................... ⬡

NDB ..............................................

Commercial broadcast station......................................... ⊙ WKBW
1520

Compass locator frequency.............................................
> **NAME**
> NAM ⊏⊐ **000**
> DME Chan 00

Localizer facility information box ...........................
> **NAME**
> NAM ⊏⊐ 000.0(T)
> DME Chan 00
> MN ⊏⊐ 000

VORTAC facility information box................ (blue)

Controlling FSS ...............
> 123.6   122.6
> 122.1 R

**FAYETTEVILLE FYV**

> 122.1 R
> WASHINGTON

Remote air/ground communications with ARTCC.............
> NAME
> Name
> 134.3   269.5

Airport with a published instrument approach ......... *(see below)*

Airport without a published instrument approach .... *(see below)*

| **AIRPORT DATA** | Airports/Seaplane bases shown in BLUE and GREEN have an approved Low Altitude Instrument Approach Procedure published. Those in BLUE have an approved DOD Low Altitude Instrument Approach Procedure and/or DOD RADAR MINIMA published in DOD FLIPS or Alaska Terminal. Airports/Seaplane bases shown in BROWN do not have a published Instrument Approach Procedure. |
|---|---|

Compass rose ...............................................................

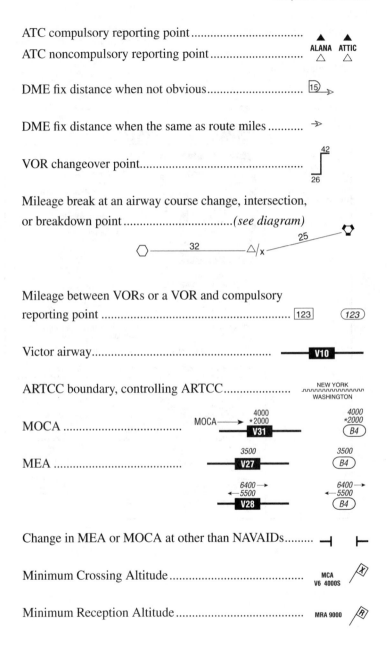

ATC compulsory reporting point ..................................

ATC noncompulsory reporting point .............................

DME fix distance when not obvious.............................

DME fix distance when the same as route miles ..........

VOR changeover point..................................................

Mileage break at an airway course change, intersection, or breakdown point ..................................*(see diagram)*

Mileage between VORs or a VOR and compulsory reporting point ...........................................................

Victor airway.......................................................

ARTCC boundary, controlling ARTCC....................

MOCA ......................................

MEA ........................................

Change in MEA or MOCA at other than NAVAIDs.........

Minimum Crossing Altitude ..........................................

Minimum Reception Altitude .........................................

Maximum Authorized Altitude....... ━MAA-15500━ ━━ V30 ━━  MAA-15500 (R5)

Magnetic variation .......................................................... ⟋⁊E⟍

Special-use airspace....................................*(see below)*

---

# AIRSPACE INFORMATION

## SPECIAL USE AIRSPACE

Only the airspace effective below 18,000 feet MSL is shown.

†P-56
W-123
A-123
REESE 1 MOA
R-1234 ①
TO 10000 ②
0600-1800Z
MON-FRI ③
IFR ④
FSS ⑤

TO 5000

A - Alert Area
P - Prohibited Area
R - Restricted Area
W - Warning Area
D - Danger Area (Canada)

Line delimits altitude separation within same Special Use Airspace Area

BROWN MOA
8000 AND ABOVE
INTERMITTENT
BY NOTAM
KANSAS CITY CENTER/FSS

Special Air Traffic Rules

MOA - Military Operations Area

†Indicates complete information in tabulation on front panel

### SPECIAL USE AIRSPACE WILL INCLUDE:

① AREA IDENTIFICATION: In Canada area ident is preceded by the letters CY (CANADA) followed by a number (PROVINCE).

② EFFECTIVE ALTITUDE CEILINGS ARE SHOWN UP TO BUT NOT INCLUDING 18,000'. WHEN THE AIRSPACE ENCOMPASSES ALL ALTITUDES IN THE LOW ALTITUDE STRUCTURE, NO ALTITUDE WILL BE SHOWN. THE WORK "TO" (AN ALTITUDE) MEANS "TO AND INCLUDING" (THAT ALTITUDE).

③ OPERATING TIME: When continuous no time is shown.
Days: Sunrise to Sunset.
Nights: Sunset to Sunrise.
Hours: Given in UTC; e.g., 0600-1300Z
Mon-Fri: Indicates area does not exist on Sat. or Sun.

1 Mar.-15 June: Indicates area in use only through dates given. By NOTAM: Area activated by NOTAM. Days are local.

④ Weather Conditions during which the area is in operation. When continuous no weather is shown.
VFR: Used only during VFR conditions. IFR: Used only during IFR conditions.

⑤ Voice Call of Controlling Agency for enroute clearance through area. No A/G unless indicated.

Class B airspace ...............................................

Class C airspace ...............................................

AIRSPACE INFORMATION

Class E airspace ..................................... Open area (white) indicates controlled airspace (Class E) unless otherwise indicated.
All airspace 14,500' and above is controlled (Class E).

Class G airspace ................................... Shaded area (brown) indicates uncontrolled airspace below 14,500' (Class G).

Mode C area ...................................................

ARTCC boundaries .................................................. ⊓⊔⊓⊔⊓⊔⊓⊔⊓⊔⊓⊔

ARTCC Remoted VHF/UHF frequency site ..........
```
    NAME
    Name
000.0    000.0
```

Air Defense Identification Zone (ADIZ) .................

HIWAS ........................................................................... **Ⓗ**

TWEB ........................................................................... **Ⓣ**

ILS localizer course with ATC function

(Airport Name)⬜D
280 Ⓛ* 43s
ATIS ............................... Automatic Terminal → (A)   *109.8
Information Service

Pilot Controlled Lighting ............................................................ Ⓛ

Special VFR not authorized .............................................. No SVFR

# I. Airspace

## 1. What is Class A airspace? (AIM 3-2-2)

Generally, that airspace from 18,000 feet MSL up to and including FL600, including airspace overlying the waters within 12 nautical miles of the coast of the 48 contiguous states and Alaska; and designated international airspace beyond 12 nautical miles of the coast of the 48 contiguous states and Alaska within areas of domestic radio navigational signal or ATC radar coverage, and within which domestic procedures are applied.

## 2. What is Class B airspace? (AIM 3-2-3)

Generally, that airspace from the surface to 10,000 feet MSL surrounding the nation's busiest airports in terms of IFR operations or passenger enplanements. The configuration of each Class B airspace area is individually tailored and consists of a surface area and two or more layers (some resemble an upside-down wedding cake), and is designated to contain all published instrument procedures once an aircraft enters the airspace. An ATC clearance is required for all aircraft to operate in the area, and all aircraft cleared as such receive separation services within the airspace. The cloud clearance requirement for VFR operations is "clear of clouds."

## 3. What is Class C airspace? (AIM 3-2-4)

Generally, that airspace from the surface to 4,000 feet above the airport elevation (charted in MSL) surrounding airports that have an operational control tower, are serviced by a radar approach control, and that have a certain number of IFR operations or passenger enplanements. Although the configuration of each Class C airspace area is individually tailored, the airspace usually consists of a 5 NM radius core surface area that extends from the surface up to 4,000 feet above the airport elevation, and a 10 NM radius shelf area that extends from 1,200 feet to 4,000 feet above the airport elevation.

### 4. What is Class D airspace? (AIM 3-2-5)

Generally, that airspace from the surface to 2,500 feet above the airport elevation (charted in MSL) surrounding airports that have an operational control tower. The configuration of each Class D airspace area is individually tailored, and when instrument procedures are published, the airspace will usually be designed to contain those procedures.

### 5. When a control tower, located at an airport within Class D airspace, ceases operation for the day, what happens to the lower limit of the controlled airspace? (AIM 3-2-5)

During the hours the tower is not in operation, Class E surface area rules, or a combination of Class E rules to 700 feet AGL and Class G rules to the surface, will become applicable. Check the A/FD for specifics.

### 6. What is Class E (controlled) airspace? (AIM 3-2-6)

Generally, if the airspace is not Class A, Class B, Class C, or Class D, and it is controlled airspace, it is Class E airspace. Class E airspace extends upward from either the surface or a designated altitude to the overlying controlled airspace. When designated as a surface area, the airspace will be configured to contain all instrument procedures. Also in this class are federal airways, airspace beginning at either 700 or 1,200 feet AGL used to transition to or from the terminal or enroute environment, enroute domestic, and offshore airspace areas designated below 18,000 feet MSL. Unless designated at a lower altitude, Class E airspace begins at 14,500 feet MSL over the United States, including that airspace overlying the waters within 12 nautical miles of the coast of the 48 contiguous states and Alaska, up to, but not including 18,000 feet MSL, and the airspace above FL600.

### 7. What is the floor of Class E airspace when designated in conjunction with an airport with an approved IAP? (14 CFR 71.71)

700 feet AGL.

**8. What is the floor of Class E airspace when designated in conjunction with a federal airway?** (14 CFR 71.71)

1,200 feet AGL.

**9. Class E airspace within the contiguous United States extends upward from either 700 feet AGL or 1,200 feet AGL, up to but not including what altitude?** (AIM 3-2-6)

Except for 18,000 feet MSL, Class E airspace has no defined vertical limit; rather, it extends upward from either the surface or a designated altitude to the overlying or adjacent controlled airspace. Unless designated at a lower altitude, Class E airspace begins at 14,500 feet MSL and extends up to, but not including 18,000 feet MSL, overlying the 48 contiguous states including the waters within 12 miles from the coast of the contiguous states.

**10. What is Class G airspace?** (AIM 3-3-1)

Class G airspace is that portion of the airspace that has not been designated as Class A, B, C, D, and E airspace.

**11. What are the vertical limits of Class G airspace?**

Class G airspace begins at the surface and continues up to but not including the overlying controlled airspace, or 14,500 MSL, or where Class E airspace begins, whichever occurs first.

# J. Special Use Airspace

## 1. Define the following types of airspace.
(AIM 3-4-1 through 3-4-7, and 3-5-7)

*Prohibited Area*—For security or other reasons, aircraft flight is prohibited.

*Restricted Area*—Contains unusual, often invisible hazards to aircraft, flights must have permission from the controlling agency, if VFR. IFR flights will be cleared through or vectored around it.

*Military Operations Area*—MOAs consist of airspace of defined vertical and lateral limits established for the purpose of separating certain military training activities from IFR traffic. Permission is not required for VFR flights, but extreme caution should be exercised. IFR flights will be cleared through or vectored around it.

*Warning Area*—Airspace of defined dimensions extending from 3 nautical miles outward from the coast of the U.S. containing activity that may be hazardous to nonparticipating aircraft. A warning area may be located over domestic or international waters or both. Permission is not required but a flight plan is advised.

*Alert Area*—Depicted on aeronautical charts to inform nonparticipating pilots of areas that may contain a high volume of pilot training or an unusual type of aerial activity. No permission is required, but VFR flights should exercise extreme caution. IFR flights will be cleared through or vectored around it.

*Controlled Firing Areas*—CFAs contain activities which, if not conducted in a controlled environment, could be hazardous to nonparticipating aircraft. These activities are suspended immediately when spotter aircraft, radar or ground lookout positions, indicate an aircraft might be approaching the area. CFAs are not charted.

*Continued*

*National Security Area*—Airspace of defined vertical and lateral dimensions established at locations where there is a requirement for increased security and safety of ground facilities. Pilots are requested to voluntarily avoid flying through the depicted NSA. When it is necessary to provide a greater level of security and safety, flight in NSAs may be temporarily prohibited by regulation under the provisions of 14 CFR §99.7.

*Temporary Flight Restrictions*—TFRs are established to protect persons and property in the air or on the surface from an existing or imminent hazard associated with an incident on the surface when the presence of low flying aircraft would magnify, alter, spread, or compound that hazard. A NOTAM designating the area within which TFRs apply and specifying the hazard or condition requiring their imposition will be issued.

## 2. Where can information on special use airspace be found? (AIM 3-4-1)

The chart legend contains information on special use airspace such as times of use, altitudes, and the controlling agency.

# Additional Study Questions

1. What does the term "pilot's discretion" mean in an ATC clearance? (P/CG)

2. Why are changeover points established? (AIM 5-3-6)

3. How are changeover points depicted on enroute charts? (AIM 5-3-6)

4. When may a pilot operate an aircraft below the published MEA? (14 CFR 91.177)

5. What procedures should be used when flying a DME arc? (FAA-H-8083-15)

6. ATC will issue speed adjustments to pilots of radar controlled aircraft. Pilots complying with speed adjustments are expected to maintain airspeed within what tolerances? (AIM 4-4-12)

7. Both communication receivers have failed. In what other way could you receive ATC instructions with cell phone or handheld radio unavailable? (FAA-H-8083-15)

# Arrival 4

# A. Approach Control

## 1. What is a STAR? (AIM 5-4-1)

A Standard Terminal Arrival Route (STAR) is an ATC-coded IFR arrival route established for use by arriving IFR aircraft destined for certain airports. Its purpose is to simplify clearance delivery procedures and facilitate transition between enroute and instrument approach procedures. Reference the Terminal Procedures Publication (TPP) for the availability of STARs.

## 2. If ATC issues your flight a STAR, must you accept it? (AIM 5-4-1)

You are not required to accept a STAR, but if you do, you must be in possession of at least the approved chart. RNAV STARs must be retrievable by the procedure name from the aircraft database and conform to the charted procedure. Pilots should notify ATC if they do not wish to use a STAR by placing "NO STAR" in the remarks section of the flight plan, or by the less desirable method of verbally stating the same to ATC.

## 3. What is an RNAV STAR? (FAA-H-8261-1)

STARs designated RNAV serve the same purpose as conventional STARs, but are only used by aircraft equipped with FMS or GPS. An RNAV STAR or STAR transition typically includes flyby waypoints, with fly-over waypoints used only when operationally required. These waypoints may be assigned crossing altitudes and speeds to optimize the descent and deceleration profiles.

## 4. When being radar-vectored for an approach, at what point may you start a descent from your last assigned altitude to a lower altitude if "cleared for the approach"? (AIM 5-5-4)

Upon receipt of an approach clearance while on an unpublished route or being radar vectored, a pilot will comply with the minimum altitude for IFR and maintain the last assigned altitude until established on a segment of a published route or IAP, at which time published altitudes apply.

## 5. Define the terms:

### Initial approach segment
### Intermediate approach segment
### Final approach segment
### Missed approach segment

(Pilot/Controller Glossary)

An instrument approach procedure may have as many as four separate segments depending upon how the approach procedure is structured.

The *initial approach segment* is that segment between the initial approach fix and the intermediate fix, or the point where the aircraft is established on the intermediate course or final approach course.

The *intermediate approach segment* is between the intermediate fix or point and the final approach fix.

The *final approach segment* is between the final approach fix or point and the runway, airport, or missed approach point.

The *missed approach segment* is between the missed approach point or the point of arrival at decision height, and the missed approach fix at the prescribed altitude.

## 6. What are standard IFR separation minimums?
(AIM 4-4-11)

When radar is employed in the separation of aircraft at the same altitude, a minimum of 3 miles separation is provided between aircraft operating within 40 miles of the radar antenna site, and 5 miles between aircraft operating beyond 40 miles from the antenna site. These minima may be increased or decreased in certain specific situations.

## 7. What is a Minimum Vectoring Altitude (MVA)?
(P/CG and AIM 5-4-5)

MVA is the lowest MSL altitude at which an IFR aircraft will be vectored by a radar controller, except as otherwise authorized for radar approaches, departures, and missed approaches. The altitude meets IFR obstacle clearance criteria. It may be lower than the published MEA along an airway or J-route segment. It may be used for radar vectoring only upon the controller's determination that an adequate radar return is being received from the aircraft being controlled. Charts depicting minimum vectoring altitudes are normally available only to the controllers and not to the pilots.

### 8. What are feeder routes? (FAA-H-8261-1)

A feeder route is a route depicted on IAP charts to designate courses for aircraft to proceed from the enroute structure to the IAF. When a feeder route is designated, the chart provides the course or bearing to be flown, the distance, and the minimum altitude. Enroute airway obstacle clearance criteria apply to feeder routes, providing 1,000 feet of obstacle clearance (2,000 feet in mountainous areas).

### 9. What procedure is to be used when the clearance "cleared for the visual" is issued? (AIM 5-4-22)

A visual approach is conducted on an IFR flight plan and authorizes a pilot to proceed visually and clear of clouds to the airport. The pilot must have either the airport or the preceding identified aircraft in sight. This approach must be authorized and controlled by the appropriate air traffic control facility. Reported weather at the airport must have a ceiling at or above 1,000 feet and visibility 3 miles or greater.

Visual approaches are an IFR procedure conducted under IFR in visual meteorological conditions. Cloud clearance requirements of 14 CFR §91.155 are not applicable.

### 10. Describe the term "contact approach." (P/CG)

An approach in which an aircraft on an IFR flight plan, having an air traffic control authorization, operating clear of clouds with at least 1 mile flight visibility and a reasonable expectation of continuing to the destination airport in those conditions, may deviate from the instrument approach procedure and proceed to the destination airport by visual reference to the surface. This approach will only be authorized when requested by the pilot and the reported ground visibility at the destination airport is at least 1 statute mile.

## 11. When is a procedure turn not required? (AIM 5-4-9)

A procedure turn is not required when:

a. The symbol "NoPT" is depicted.

b. "Radar Vectoring" is provided.

c. A holding pattern is published in lieu of a procedure turn.

d. Conducting a timed approach.

e. The procedure turn is not authorized (absence of procedure turn barb on plan view).

## 12. What are standard procedure turn limitations? (AIM 5-4-9)

a. Turn on the depicted side.

b. Adhere to depicted minimum altitudes.

c. Complete the maneuver within the distance specified in the profile view.

d. Maneuver at a maximum speed not greater than 200 knots (IAS).

## 13. What procedure is followed when a holding pattern is specified in lieu of a procedure turn? (AIM 5-4-9)

A holding pattern, in lieu of a procedure turn, may be specified for course reversal in some procedures: the holding pattern is established over an intermediate fix or final approach fix. The holding pattern distance or time specified in the profile view must be observed. Maximum holding airspeed limitations apply, as set forth for all holding patterns. The holding pattern maneuver is completed when the aircraft is established on the inbound course after executing the appropriate entry. If cleared for the approach prior to returning to the holding fix, and the aircraft is at the prescribed altitude, additional circuits of the holding pattern are not necessary nor expected by ATC. If pilots elect to make additional circuits to lose altitude or to become better established on course, it is their responsibility to so advise ATC upon receipt of their approach clearance.

# B. Precision Approaches

## 1. What is a precision approach (PA)? (AIM 5-4-5)

A precision approach (PA) is an instrument approach that is based on a navigation system that provides course and glidepath deviation information meeting the precision standards of ICAO Annex 10. For example, PAR, ILS, and GLS are precision approaches.

## 2. What are the basic components of a standard ILS? (AIM 1-1-9)

Guidance information ..................... localizer, glide slope

Range information .......................... marker beacons, DME

Visual information .......................... approach lights, touchdown and centerline lights, runway lights

## 3. Describe both visual and aural indications that a pilot would receive when crossing the outer, middle, and inner markers of a standard ILS. (AIM 1-1-9)

| **Outer Marker** | **Middle Marker** | **Inner Marker** |
|---|---|---|
| blue light | amber light | white light |
| dull tone | medium tone | high tone |
| slow speed | medium speed | high speed |
| − − − − − − | − . − . − . | . . . . . . |

## 4. What are the distances from the landing threshold of the outer, middle, and inner markers? (AIM 1-1-9)

Outer marker ....................... 4 to 7 miles from threshold

Middle marker .................... 3,500 feet from threshold

Inner marker....................... between middle marker and threshold

## 5. When is the inner marker used? (AIM 1-1-9)

Ordinarily, there are two marker beacons associated with an ILS, the outer marker (OM) and middle marker (MM). Locations with a Category II ILS also have an inner marker (IM).

6. **To maintain glide slope and desired airspeed on an ILS approach, how are power and pitch used?**

   When on the final segment of an ILS final approach, change pitch to control glide path, and change power to control airspeed.

7. **While flying a 3° glide slope, which conditions should the pilot expect concerning airspeed, pitch attitude and altitude when encountering a windshear situation where a tailwind shears to a calm or headwind?** (AC 00-54)

   Pitch attitude ......................... Increase
   Required thrust ...................... Reduced, then increased
   Vertical speed ........................ Decreases, then increases
   Airspeed ............................... Increases, then decreases
   Reaction ............................... Reduce power initially, then increase

8. **While flying a 3° glide slope, which conditions should the pilot expect concerning airspeed, pitch attitude, and altitude when encountering a windshear situation where a headwind shears to a calm or tailwind?** (AC 00-54)

   Pitch attitude .................................. Decrease
   Required thrust .............................. Increased, then reduced
   Vertical speed ................................ Increases
   Airspeed ....................................... Decreases, then increases
   Reaction ....................................... Increased power, then a
   decrease in power

9. **Localizers operate within what frequency range?** (AIM 1-1-9)

   Localizers operate on odd tenths within the 108.10 to 111.95 MHz band.

10. **Where is the localizer/transmitter antenna installation located in relation to the runway?** (AIM 1-1-9)

    The antenna is located at the far end of the approach runway.

**11. Where is the glide slope antenna located and what is its normal usable range?** (AIM 1-1-9)

The glide slope transmitter is located between 750 feet and 1,250 feet from the approach end of the runway (down the runway), and offset 250 feet to 650 feet from it. The glide slope is normally usable to a distance of 10 NM.

**12. What range does a standard localizer have?** (AIM 1-1-9)

The localizer signal provides course guidance throughout the descent path to the runway threshold from a distance of 18 NM from the antenna site.

**13. What is the angular width of a localizer signal?** (AIM 1-1-9)

The localizer signal is adjusted to provide an angular width of between 3° to 6°, as necessary to provide a linear width of 700 feet at the runway approach threshold.

**14. What is the normal glide slope angle for a standard ILS?** (AIM 1-1-9)

The glide path projection angle is normally 3 degrees above horizontal so that it intersects the MM at about 200 feet and the OM at about 1,400 feet above the runway elevation.

**15. What is the sensitivity of a CDI tuned to a localizer signal compared with a CDI tuned to a VOR?** (FAA-H-8083-15)

Full left or full right deflection occurs at approximately 2.5° from the centerline of a localizer course, which is 4 times greater than when tuned to a VOR, where full-scale deflection equals 10° from the centerline.

**16. Define the term "decision height" (DH).** (P/CG)

With respect to the operation of an aircraft, decision height means the height at which a decision must be made, during an ILS, MLS, or PAR instrument approach to either continue the approach or execute a missed approach.

## 17. When flying an instrument approach procedure, when can the pilot descend below the MDA or DH? (14 CFR 91.175)

No person may operate an aircraft below the prescribed MDA or continue an approach below the authorized DH unless:

a. The aircraft is continuously in a position from which a descent to a landing on the intended runway can be made at a normal rate of descent using normal maneuvers.

b. The flight visibility is not less than the visibility prescribed in the standard instrument approach procedure being used.

c. When at least one of the following visual references for the intended runway is distinctly visible and identifiable to the pilot:

   • The approach light system, (except that the pilot may not descend below 100 feet above the touchdown zone elevation using the ALS as a reference unless the red terminating bars or the red side row bars are also distinctly visible and identifiable)

   • The threshold

   • The threshold markings

   • The threshold lights

   • REIL

   • VASI

   • The touchdown zone markings

   • The touchdown zone lights

   • The runway and runway markings

   • The runway lights

## 18. What are the legal substitutions for an inoperative outer marker? (14 CFR 91.175)

Compass locator; precision approach radar (PAR) or airport surveillance radar (ASR); DME, VOR, or NDB fixes authorized in the standard instrument approach procedure; or a suitable RNAV system in conjunction with a fix identified in the standard instrument approach procedure.

**19. What are PAR and ASR approaches?** (AIM 5-4-11)

A PAR approach is a type of radar approach in which a controller provides highly accurate navigational guidance in azimuth and elevation to the pilot (precision approach). An ASR approach is a type of radar approach in which a controller provides navigational guidance in azimuth only (nonprecision approach).

**20. What is a "no-gyro" approach?** (P/CG and AIM 5-4-11)

A "no-gyro" approach is a radar approach/vector provided in case of a malfunctioning gyro-compass or directional gyro. Instead of providing the pilot with headings to be flown, the controller observes the radar track and issues control instructions "Turn right/ left," or "Stop turn," as appropriate.

**21. What rate of turn is recommended during execution of a "no-gyro" approach procedure?** (AIM 5-4-11)

On a no-gyro approach, all turns should be standard rate until on final; then one-half standard rate on final approach.

**22. If conducting an ASR approach, are the minimums expressed as DH or MDA?** (AIM 5-4-11)

An ASR approach is a nonprecision approach with no glide slope provided; minimums are depicted as MDA.

## C. Nonprecision Approaches

**1. What is the definition of the term "nonprecision approach"?** (AIM 5-4-5)

A nonprecision approach (NPA) is an instrument approach based on a navigation system that provides course deviation information, but no glidepath deviation information such as VOR, NDB and LNAV.

**2. Name the types of nonprecision approach procedures available.** (P/CG)

The types of nonprecision approaches available are VOR, TACAN, NDB, LOC, ASR, LDA, and SDF.

### 3. Define MDA. (P/CG)

The Minimum Descent Altitude is the lowest altitude, expressed in feet above MSL, to which descent is authorized on final approach or during circle-to-land maneuvering, in execution of a standard instrument approach procedure where no electronic glide slope is provided.

### 4. Define VDP. (P/CG)

*Visual Descent Point*—a VDP is a defined point on the final approach course of a nonprecision straight-in approach procedure from which normal descent from the MDA to the runway touchdown point may be commenced, provided the approach threshold of that runway, or approach lights or other markings identifiable with the approach end of that runway, are clearly visible to the pilot. Pilots not equipped to receive the VDP should fly the approach procedure as though no VDP had been provided. On an approach chart, a VDP is identified in the profile view by a "V."

### 5. What is a "VDA"? (AIM 5-4-5)

On nonprecision approaches, Vertical Descent Angle (VDA) describes a computed path from the final approach fix (FAF) and altitude to the runway threshold at the published Threshold Crossing Height (TCH). The optimum descent angle is 3.00 degrees and, whenever possible, the approach will be designed to accommodate this angle. It provides the means for the pilot to establish a stabilized approach descent from the FAF or stepdown fix to the TCH. Pilots can use the published angle and estimated/actual groundspeed to find a target rate of descent from a table published in the back of the TPP. The FAA will eventually publish VDAs on all nonprecision approaches.

### 6. Will standard instrument approach procedures always have a final approach fix (FAF)? (FAA-H-8261-1)

No. When a FAF is not designated, such as on an approach that incorporates an on-airport VOR or NDB, a final approach point is designated and is typically where the procedure turn intersects the final approach course inbound.

**7. If no FAF is published, where does the final approach segment begin on a nonprecision approach?** (Order 8260.3B TERPs)

The final approach segment begins where the procedure turn intersects the final approach course inbound.

**8. Certain conditions are required for an instrument approach procedure to have "straight-in" minimums published. What are they?** (AIM 5-4-20)

Straight-in minimums are shown on the IAP when the final approach course is within 30 degrees of the runway alignment (15 degrees for GPS IAPs) and a normal descent can be made from the IFR altitude shown on the IAP to the runway surface.

**9. What is a stepdown fix?** (P/CG)

A stepdown fix permits additional descent within a segment of an instrument approach procedure by identifying a point at which a controlling obstacle has been safely overflown.

**10. What does a VASI system provide?** (AIM 2-1-2)

A VASI system provides visual descent guidance during an approach to a runway; safe obstruction clearance within ±10° of extended runway centerline up to 4 NM from the runway threshold. Two-bar VASI installations normally provide a 3° visual glide path.

**11. What are the major differences between SDF and LDA approaches?** (FAA-H-8083-15)

In an SDF approach procedure, the SDF course may or may not be aligned with the runway; usable off-course indications are limited to 35° either side of course centerline. The SDF signal emitted is fixed at either 6° or 12°.

The LDA compares in utility and accuracy to a localizer, but it is not part of a complete ILS. The LDA course width is between 3° and 6° and thus provides a more precise approach course than an SDF installation. Some LDAs are equipped with a GS. The LDA course is not aligned with the runway, but straight-in minimums may be published where the angle between the runway centerline and the LDA course does not exceed 30°. If this angle exceeds 30°, only circling minimums are published.

## 12. What criteria determines whether or not you may attempt an approach? (14 CFR 91.175)

No regulation states that you cannot attempt an approach, if operating under Part 91 regulations. But if you reach MDA or DH and decide to descend to land, flight visibility must be at least equal to that published.

## 13. What regulations require use of specified procedures by all pilots approaching for landing under IFR? (14 CFR Part 97)

Specified procedures are required by 14 CFR Part 97.

# D. RNAV (GPS) Approaches

## 1. What are several types of GPS approach procedures in use? (FAA-H-8261-1)

a. GPS overlay of pre-existing nonprecision approaches.

b. VOR/DME based RNAV approaches.

c. Stand-alone RNAV (GPS) approaches.

d. RNAV (GPS) approaches with vertical guidance (APV).

e. RNAV (GPS) precision approaches (WAAS and LAAS).

## 2. What is the GPS overlay program? (AIM 1-1-19)

The GPS Approach Overlay Program is an authorization for pilots to use GPS avionics under IFR for flying designated nonprecision instrument approach procedures, except LOC, LDA, and SDF procedures. These procedures are now identified by the name of the procedure and "or GPS" (e.g., VOR/DME or GPS RWY 15). Only approaches contained in the current onboard navigation database are authorized.

## 3. What is a GPS stand-alone approach? (AC 90-94)

A GPS stand-alone approach consists of a sequence of waypoints defining the point-to-point track to be flown coded into the database, including the initial approach, intermediate, final approach, missed approach, missed approach turning, and missed approach

holding waypoints. All waypoints, except a missed approach
waypoint at the runway threshold, will be named with a five-letter
alpha character name. Missed approach waypoints at the threshold
will be assigned a database identifier. The sequence of waypoints
appearing in the display should be identical to the waypoint
sequence appearing on an associated approach chart.

### 4. What is a TAA with regard to GPS approaches?
(AIM 5-4-5)

Terminal Arrival Area is controlled airspace established in conjunction with the standard or modified RNAV approach configurations. It provides a seamless transition from the enroute structure to
the terminal environment for arriving aircraft equipped with FMS
and/or GPS navigational equipment. The TAA provides a NoPT for
aircraft using the approach and has three standard areas: straight-
in, left base, and right base. The arc boundaries of the three areas
are published portions of the approach and allow aircraft to transition from the en route structure direct to the nearest IAF.

### 5. When flying a GPS approach, is it necessary to monitor ground-based NAVAIDs as a backup to the GPS equipment? (AIM 1-1-19)

Many of the original overlay approaches have been replaced with
stand-alone procedures specifically designed for use by GPS systems. The title of the remaining GPS overlay procedures has been
revised on the approach chart to "or GPS" (e.g., VOR or GPS
RWY 24). Therefore, all the approaches that can be used by GPS
now contain "GPS" in the title (e.g., "VOR or GPS RWY 24,"
"GPS RWY 24," or "RNAV (GPS) RWY 24"). During these GPS
approaches, underlying ground-based NAVAIDs are not required
to be operational and associated aircraft avionics need not be
installed, operational, turned on or monitored (monitoring of the
underlying approach is suggested when equipment is available
and functional). Existing overlay approaches may be requested
using the GPS title, such as "GPS RWY 24" for the VOR or GPS
RWY 24.

6. **When can RNAV equipment be used as a substitute means of navigation guidance?** (AIM 1-2-3)

   Suitable RNAV systems (TSO-C129/-C145/-C146) may be used in the following ways:

   a. Determine aircraft position over or distance from a VOR, TACAN, NDB, compass locator, DME fix; or a named fix defined by a VOR radial, TACAN course, NDB bearing, or compass locator bearing intersecting a VOR or localizer course.

   b. Navigate to or from a VOR, TACAN, NDB, or compass locator.

   c. Hold over a VOR, TACAN, NDB, compass locator, or DME fix.

   d. Fly an arc based upon DME.

   *Note:* These operations are allowable even when a facility is explicitly identified as required on a procedure (e.g., "Note ADF required"). Also, these operations do not include navigation on localizer-based courses (including localizer back-course guidance).

7. **What restrictions apply to the use of GPS as a substitute for ADF and/or DME?** (AIM 1-1-19)

   Waypoints, fixes, intersections, and facility locations to be used for these operations must be retrieved from the GPS airborne database. The database must be current. If the required positions cannot be retrieved from the airborne database, the substitution of GPS for ADF and/or DME is not authorized.

8. **If flying a VOR/DME approach without operative DME onboard, could you use GPS info in lieu of DME info?** (AIM 1-1-19)

   When using a facility as the active waypoint, the only acceptable facility is the DME facility which is charted as the one used to establish the DME fix. If this facility is not in your airborne database, you are not authorized to use a facility waypoint for this operation.

## 9. What restrictions apply concerning filing an airport as an alternate when using GPS? (AIM 1-1-19, FAA-H-8083-15)

Any required alternate airport must have an approved instrument approach procedure other than GPS that is anticipated to be operational and available at the estimated time of arrival, and which the aircraft is equipped to fly. If the non-GPS approaches on which the pilot must rely require DME or ADF, the aircraft must be equipped with DME or ADF avionics as appropriate.

## 10. What is "WAAS"? (P/CG)

Wide-area augmentation system (WAAS) is a satellite navigation system consisting of the equipment and software which augments the GPS Standard Positioning Service (SPS). The WAAS provides enhanced integrity, accuracy, availability, and continuity over and above GPS SPS. The differential correction function provides improved accuracy required for precision approach. Aircraft equipped with an approved WAAS receiver can use GPS as the primary navigation system from takeoff through a Category 1 precision approach.

## 11. What does "APV" mean? (AIM 1-1-20)

Approach with Vertical Guidance is a new class of approach procedures that provides vertical guidance, but does not meet the ICAO Annex 10 requirements for precision approaches. These new procedures are defined in ICAO Annex 6, and include approaches such as the LNAV/VNAV procedures presently being flown with barometric vertical navigation (Baro-VNAV). These approaches provide vertical guidance, but do not meet the more stringent standards of a precision approach. Properly certified WAAS receivers will be able to fly these LNAV/VNAV procedures using a WAAS electronic glide path, which eliminates the errors that can be introduced by using barometric altimetry.

## 12. What does "LPV" mean? (AIM 1-1-20)

Localizer Performance with Vertical Guidance is a new type of APV approach procedure, in addition to LNAV/VNAV, which takes advantage of the high accuracy guidance and increased integrity provided by WAAS. This angular guidance allows the use of TERPs approach criteria used for ILS approaches. The resulting approach procedure minima ("LPV") may have decision altitudes as low as 200 feet height above touchdown with visibility minimums as low as $\frac{1}{2}$ mile, when the terrain and airport infrastructure support the lowest minima. LPV minima are published on the RNAV (GPS) approach charts.

## 13. How can you determine if your aircraft is equipped to fly an LPV approach procedure? (AIM 1-1-20)

Receivers capable of flying LP procedures must contain a statement in the Flight Manual Supplement or Approved Supplemental Flight Manual stating that the receiver has LP capability, as well as the capability for the other WAAS and GPS approach procedure types.

# E. Circling Approaches

## 1. What are circle-to-land approaches? (P/CG)

A circle-to-land approach is not technically an approach, but a maneuver initiated by a pilot to align the aircraft with the runway for landing when a straight-in landing from an instrument approach is not possible or desirable. At tower-controlled airports, this maneuver is made only after ATC authorization has been obtained and the pilot has established required visual reference to the airport.

## 2. Why do certain airports have only circling minimums published? (AIM 5-4-20)

When either the normal rate of descent or the runway alignment factor of 30 degrees (15 degrees for GPS IAPs) is exceeded, a straight-in minimum is not published and a circling minimum applies.

### 3. Can a pilot make a straight-in landing if using an approach procedure having only circling minimums? (AIM 5-4-20)

Yes; the fact that a straight-in minimum is not published does not preclude pilots from landing straight-in, if they have the active runway in sight and have sufficient time to make a normal approach to landing. Under such conditions and when ATC has cleared them for landing on that runway, pilots are not expected to circle, even though only circling minimums are published.

### 4. If cleared for a "straight-in VOR-DME 34 approach," can a pilot circle to land, if needed? (P/CG)

Yes. A "straight-in approach" is an instrument approach wherein final approach is begun without first having executed a procedure turn. Such an approach is not necessarily completed with a straight-in landing or made to straight-in minimums.

### 5. When can you begin your descent to the runway during a circling approach? (14 CFR 91.175)

Three conditions are required before descent from the MDA can occur:

a.  The aircraft is continuously in a position from which a descent to a landing on the intended runway can be made at a normal rate of descent using normal maneuvers.

b.  The flight visibility is not less than the visibility prescribed in the standard instrument approach being used.

c.  At least one of the specific runway visual references for the intended runway is distinctly visible and identifiable to the pilot.

**6. While circling to land you lose visual contact with the runway environment. At the time visual contact is lost, your approximate position is a base leg at the circling MDA. What procedure should be followed?** (AIM 5-4-21)

If visual reference is lost while circling to land from an instrument approach, the pilot should make an initial climbing turn toward the landing runway and continue the turn until established on the missed approach course. Since the circling maneuver may be accomplished in more than one direction, different patterns will be required to become established on the prescribed missed approach course, depending on the aircraft position at the time visual reference is lost. Adherence to the procedure will ensure that an aircraft will remain within the circling and missed approach obstacle clearance areas.

**7. What obstacle clearance are you guaranteed during a circling approach maneuver?** (FAA-H-8083-15)

In all circling approaches, the circling minimum provides 300 feet of obstacle clearance within the circling approach area. The size of this area depends on the category in which the aircraft operates.

Category A ..................................... 1.3-mile radius
Category B ..................................... 1.5-mile radius
Category C ..................................... 1.7-mile radius
Category D ..................................... 2.3-mile radius
Category E ..................................... 4.5-mile radius

**8. How can a pilot determine the approach category minimums applicable to a particular aircraft?** (AIM 5-4-7)

Minimums are specified for various aircraft approach categories based on a speed of $V_{REF}$, if specified, or if $V_{REF}$ is not specified, 1.3 $V_{SO}$ at the maximum certificated gross landing weight.

**9. What are the different aircraft approach categories?**
(AIM 5-4-7)

Category A ...................................... Speed less than 91 knots

Category B ...................................... Speed 91 knots or more but
less than 121 knots

Category C ...................................... Speed 121 knots or more but
less than 141 knots

Category D...................................... Speed 141 knots or more but
less than 166 knots

Category E ...................................... Speed 166 knots or more

**10. An aircraft operating under 14 CFR Part 91 has a 1.3 times $V_{SO}$ speed of 100 KIAS, making Category B minimums applicable. If it becomes necessary to circle at a speed in excess of this category, what minimums should be used?** (AIM 5-4-7)

An aircraft can only fit into one approach category. If it is necessary to maneuver at speeds in excess of the upper limit of the speed range for each category, the minimum for the next higher approach category should be used.

## F. Missed Approaches

**1. When must a pilot execute a missed approach?**
(AIM 5-4-21; 5-5-5)

A missed approach must be executed when one of the following conditions occurs:

a. Arrival at the missed approach point and the runway environment is not yet in sight;

b. Arrival at DH on the glide slope with the runway environment not yet in sight;

c. Anytime a pilot determines a safe landing is not possible;

d. When circling-to-land visual contact is lost; or

e. When instructed by ATC.

**2. On a nonprecision approach procedure, how is the Missed Approach Point (MAP) determined?** (FAA-H-8083-15)

In nonprecision procedures, the pilot determines the MAP by timing from FAF when the approach aid is well away from the airport, by a fix or NAVAID when the navigation facility is located on the field, or by waypoints as defined by GPS or VOR/DME RNAV.

**3. If no final approach fix is depicted, how is the MAP determined?** (FAA-H-8083-15)

The MAP is at the airport (NAVAID on airport).

**4. Where is the MAP on a precision approach?** (FAA-H-8083-15)

For the ILS, the MAP is at the decision altitude/decision height (DA/DH).

**5. Under what conditions are missed approach procedures published on an approach chart not followed?** (FAA-H-8083-15)

They are not followed when ATC has assigned alternate missed approach instructions.

**6. If, during the execution of an instrument approach procedure, you determine a missed approach is necessary due to full-scale needle deflection, what action is recommended?** (AIM 5-4-21)

Protected obstacle clearance areas for missed approach are predicated on the assumption that the missed approach is initiated at the decision altitude/height (DA/H) or at the missed approach point, and not lower than minimum descent altitude (MDA). Reasonable buffers are provided for normal maneuvers. However, no consideration is given to an abnormally early turn. Therefore when an early missed approach is executed, pilots should (unless otherwise cleared by ATC) fly the IAP as specified on the approach plate to the missed approach point at or above the MDA or DA/H, before executing a turning maneuver.

7. **What is the recommended action to take if it becomes necessary to execute a missed approach after passing the missed approach point on an approach?** (AIM 5-4-21)

Missed approach obstacle clearance is predicated on beginning the missed approach procedure at the Missed Approach Point (MAP) from MDA or DA and then climbing 200 feet/NM or greater. Initiating a go-around after passing the published MAP may result in total loss of obstacle clearance. To compensate for the possibility of reduced obstacle clearance during a go-around, a pilot should apply procedures used in takeoff planning. Refer to airport obstacle and departure data in the *U.S. Terminal Procedures* publication prior to initiating an instrument approach procedure.

8. **What is a low approach?** (AIM 4-3-12)

A low approach (sometimes referred to as a low pass) is the go-around maneuver following an approach. Instead of landing or making a touch and go, a pilot may wish to go-around (low approach) in order to expedite a particular operation (a series of practice instrument approaches is an example). Unless otherwise authorized by ATC, the low approach should be made straight ahead, with no turns or climb made until the pilot has made a thorough visual check for other aircraft in the area.

9. **What does the phrase "Cleared for the Option" mean?** (AIM 4-3-22)

The "Cleared for the Option" procedure will permit an instructor, flight examiner or pilot the option to make a touch-and-go, low approach, missed approach, stop-and-go, or full stop landing. The pilot should make a request for this procedure passing the final approach fix inbound on an instrument approach.

# G. Landing Procedures

**1. Is it legal to land a civil aircraft if the actual visibility is below the minimums published on the approach chart?** (14 CFR 91.175)

No, 14 CFR Part 91 states that no pilot operating an aircraft, except a military aircraft of the U.S., may land that aircraft when the flight visibility is less than the visibility prescribed in the standard instrument approach procedure being used.

**2. When landing at an airport with an operating control tower following an IFR flight, must the pilot call FSS to close the flight plan?** (AIM 5-1-14)

No, if operating on an IFR flight plan to an airport with a functioning control tower, the flight plan will automatically be closed upon landing.

**3. You are operating on an IFR flight plan into an airport without an operating control tower, and have forgotten to close your flight plan after landing. Discuss the effect this will have on ATC.** (AIM 5-1-14)

The airspace surrounding that airport cannot be released for use by other IFR aircraft until the status of your flight has been determined.

**4. If the visibility provided by ATC is less than that prescribed for the approach, can a pilot legally continue an approach and land?** (FAA-H-8083-15)

According to 14 CFR Part 91, no pilot may land when the flight visibility is less than the visibility prescribed in the standard IAP being used. ATC will provide the pilot with the current visibility reports appropriate to the runway in use. This may be in the form of prevailing visibility, runway visual value (RVV), or runway visual range (RVR). However, only the pilot can determine if the flight visibility meets the landing requirements indicated on the approach chart. If the flight visibility meets the minimum prescribed for the approach, then the approach may be continued to a landing. If the flight visibility is less than that prescribed for the approach, then the pilot must execute a missed approach, regardless of the reported visibility.

# H. Logging Flight Time

### 1. What conditions are necessary for a pilot to log instrument time? (14 CFR 61.51)

A pilot may log as instrument flight time only that time during which he/she operates the aircraft solely by reference to instruments, under actual or simulated flight conditions.

### 2. When two or more straight-in approaches with the same type of guidance exist for a runway, how will they be designated in the approach title? (FAA-H-8261-1)

A letter suffix is added to the title of the approach so that it can be more easily identified. These approach charts start with the letter Z and continue in reverse alphabetical order. Although these two approaches can both be flown with GPS to the same runway they are significantly different (in minimums, missed approach, etc.). The approach procedure labeled Z will have lower landing minimums than Y (some older charts may not reflect this). Example: RNAV (GPS) Z RWY 13C and RNAV (RNP) Y RWY 13C at MDW (Chicago Midway).

### 3. When logging instrument time, what should be included in each entry? (14 CFR 61.51)

Each entry must include the place and type of each instrument approach completed, and the name of the safety pilot (if applicable).

### 4. What conditions must exist in order to log "actual" instrument flight time?

The FAA has never defined the term "actual" instrument time. 14 CFR Part 61 defines "instrument flight time" as that flight time when a person operates an aircraft solely by reference to instruments under actual or simulated instrument flight conditions. A reasonable guideline for determining when to log "actual instrument time" would be any flight time that is accumulated in IMC conditions with flight being conducted solely by reference to instruments. The definition of IMC is weather conditions below the VFR minimums specified for visual meteorological conditions. VFR minimums are found in 14 CFR §91.155.

**5. What is the definition of "flight time"?** (14 CFR Part 1)

Flight time means pilot time that commences when an aircraft moves under its own power for the purpose of flight and ends when the aircraft comes to rest after landing.

# I. Instrument Approach Procedure Charts: General

*All questions in this section reference government NOAA charts.*

**1. If a particular approach name has a letter "A" attached as a suffix (such as VOR DME A), what does this indicate?** (FAA-H-8083-15)

A letter after the approach name indicates that the approach does not meet straight-in criteria and only circling minimums are available.

**2. Do all standard instrument approach procedures have final approach fixes?** (FAA-H-8083-15)

No, some nonprecision approaches may not have a final approach fix. These particular approaches usually have the NAVAID upon which the approach is based located on the airport.

**3. With no FAF available, when would final descent to the published MDA be started?** (FAA-H-8083-15)

When flying the full procedure, this is usually started upon completion of the procedure turn and when established on the final approach course inbound. When being radar-vectored to the final approach course, descent shall be accomplished when within the specified distance from the NAVAID and established on the inbound course.

**4. What significance does a black triangle with a white "A" appearing in the Notes section of an approach chart, have to a pilot?** (FAA-H-8083-15, TERPs)

It indicates that nonstandard IFR alternate minimums exist for the airport. If an "NA" appears after the "A," alternate minimums are not authorized. This information is found in the beginning of the TPP. Approved terminal weather observation and reporting facilities, or a general area weather report, must be available before an airport may serve as an alternate.

**5. What is the significance of the term "radar required" found on some approach charts?** (P/CG)

A term displayed on charts and approach plates and included in FDC NOTAMs to alert pilots that segments of either an instrument approach procedure or a route are not navigable because of either the absence or unusability of a NAVAID. The pilot can expect to be provided radar navigational guidance while transiting segments labeled with this term.

*The following questions are in reference to the ILS 16L approach chart for Fort Worth, Texas, depicted on Page 4–34 (NACO effective date September 6, 2001).*

# J. Instrument Approach Procedure Charts: Plan View

**1. What are the MSAs for this approach?** (FAA-H-8083-15)

2,200 feet ........................................ 180° through 270°
3,400 feet ........................................ 270° through 360°
2,800 feet ........................................ 360° through 180°

**2. On which facility is the MSA centered, and what does it provide?** (AIM 5-4-5)

The MSA is centered on the MUFIN LOM; the altitude shown provides at least 1,000 feet of clearance above the highest obstacle within the defined sector up to a distance of 25 NM from the facility. Navigational course guidance is not assured at the MSA.

3. **What is the IAF for this procedure?** (FAA-H-8083-15)

   The IAF is MUFIN LOM.

4. **What significance does the bold arrow extending from Bowie VOR have?** (FAA-H-8083-15)

   It represents a feeder route or flyable route utilized when transitioning from the enroute structure to the initial approach fix.

5. **When intercepting the localizer from procedure turn inbound, what will be the relative bearing on the ADF indicator as the localizer needle begins to center?** (FAA-H-8083-15)

   Assuming a 45° intercept angle, the relative bearing will be 315°.

6. **What are the frequencies for the locator outer marker and middle marker beacons?** (FAA-H-8083-15)

   The locator frequency is 365 kHz. All marker beacons transmit on a frequency of 75 MHz.

7. **What significance does the ring labeled "10 NM" and centered on the MUFIN LOM have?** (FAA-H-8083-15)

   The ring, normally a 10 NM radius, provides the boundary to scale of the procedure that is charted.

8. **Where does the final approach segment begin for the ILS 16L approach?** (FAA-H-8083-15)

   On all precision approaches, the final approach segment begins when the glide slope is intercepted at glide slope altitude. For non-precision approaches such as the straight-in LOC 16L approach, the final approach segment begins at the Maltese cross which is the MUFIN LOM.

# K. Instrument Approach Procedure Charts: Profile

## 1. Within what distance from the MUFIN LOM must the procedure turn be executed? (FAA-H-8083-15)

The procedure turn must be executed within 10 NM.

## 2. If a procedure turn is required, what would be the minimum altitude while flying this segment? (FAA-H-8083-15)

The minimum altitude for the initial approach segment and while executing the procedure turn is 2,300 feet MSL.

## 3. To what altitude may a pilot descend after the procedure turn? (FAA-H-8083-15)

When established inbound after the procedure turn, the pilot may descend to 2,000 MSL.

## 4. What does the number "1991" located at the outer marker indicate? (FAA-H-8083-15)

1991 indicates the altitude of the glide slope at the outer marker.

## 5. What is the glide slope angle for this approach? (FAA-H-8083-15)

The glide slope angle is 3°.

## 6. What is the altitude at which the electronic glide slope crosses the threshold of runway 16L? (FAA-H-8083-15)

Threshold crossing height (TCH) is 57 feet.

**7. If the glide slope became inoperative, could you continue this approach if established on the localizer at the time of the malfunction? Why?** (FAA-H-8083-15)

Yes, provided ATC is notified and approves a localizer-only approach. Since the procedure indicates a localizer-only minimum, a localizer-only approach can be authorized. The minimum is now an MDA and the approach is now a nonprecision procedure with MAP being a time or DME point.

**8. If you discovered your marker beacon receiver was inoperative, what are the authorized substitutes for the MUFIN outer marker?** (FAA-H-8083-15)

Substitutes for the outer marker are:

a. The compass locator (365 kHz)

b. 5.3 DME I-FTW

c. Maverick VORTAC (TTT) radial 269

**9. What DME distance is indicated in the profile view for the MUFIN LOM and the runway threshold?** (FAA-H-8083-15)

The MUFIN LOM is 5.3 NM, and the runway threshold is 1.5 NM from the localizer antenna site.

**10. Where is the MAP for the precision and nonprecision approach in this procedure?** (FAA-H-8083-15)

a. For the precision approach procedure, the MAP is upon reaching the DH of 910 feet MSL on the glide slope.

b. For the nonprecision procedure, the MAP is:

- 1.5 DME from IFTW; or
- Time from MUFIN.

# L. Instrument Approach Procedure Charts: Minimums

**1. What is the minimum visibility for a Category A full ILS 16L approach?** (FAA-H-8083-15)

Minimum visibility is $\frac{1}{2}$ mile or RVR of 2,400 feet.

**2. If the approach light system became inoperative, how would you determine the minimum visibility for a Category A full ILS 16L approach?** (FAA-H-8083-15)

To determine landing minimums when components or aids of the system are inoperative or are not utilized, inoperative components or visual aids tables are published and normally appear in the front section of NOAA approach chart books.

**3. Convert the following RVR values to meteorological visibility.** (14 CFR 91.175)

| RVR (feet) | Statute miles |
|---|---|
| 1,600 | 1/4 |
| 2,400 | 1/2 |
| 3,200 | 5/8 |
| 4,000 | 3/4 |
| 4,500 | 7/8 |
| 5,000 | 1 |
| 6,000 | 1-1/4 |

**4. Are takeoff minimums standard or nonstandard for Ft. Worth Meacham Field?** (FAA-H-8083-15)

Nonstandard; takeoff minimums are not standard and/or departure procedures are published as indicated by the triangle with a "T" printed in the notes area. The appropriate section in the front of the Terminal Procedures publication should be consulted.

**5. For the localizer approach 16L, what are the minimums for a Category A airplane if a circling maneuver is desired?** (FAA-H-8083-15)

The circling MDA is 1,260 MSL; the visibility requirement increases to 1 mile for the circling maneuver.

## 6. What significance do the numbers in parentheses (200-½) have? (FAA-H-8083-15)

Any minimums found in parentheses are not applicable to civil pilots. These minimums are directed at military pilots who should refer to appropriate regulations.

## 7. When established at the MDA on the final approach course inbound for the straight-in LOC 16L approach, is the MDA expressed as Height Above Touchdown (HAT) or Height Above Airport (HAA)? (FAA-H-8083-15)

The MDA of 530 feet for a straight-in landing always represents height above touchdown (HAT) since the approach is for a specific runway. MDAs for circling approaches will always represent height above airport (HAA) since a specific runway will not be used for landing.

## 8. What is the difference between decision altitude and decision height? (FAA-H-8083-15)

Precision approaches use decision altitude (DA), charted in "feet MSL," followed by the decision height (DH) which is referenced to the height above threshold elevation (HAT).

## 9. What do the terms LNAV and VNAV mean when indicated in the minimums section? (AIM 5-4-5)

These terms are found on RNAV (GPS) type approaches and indicate an instrument approach with lateral and/or vertical guidance. LNAV-only approaches will depict minimum altitude as MDA and LNAV/VNAV minimums will be depicted as decision altitude (DA).

## 10. If the current weather reports indicate ceilings 100 overcast and visibility ½ mile, can a pilot legally make an approach to ILS 16L, and can he land? (FAA-H-8083-15)

Under 14 CFR Part 91, the approach may be attempted regardless of the ceiling and visibility. At the DH the pilot must have the runway environment in sight and have the prescribed flight visibility to land. If these conditions are met, the approach may be continued to a landing.

# M. Instrument Approach Procedure Charts: Aerodrome

### 1. What types of lighting are available for runway 16L? (FAA-H-8083-15)

HIRL—High-intensity runway lighting

MALSR—Medium-intensity approach lighting system with sequenced flashing lights; denoted by the circled A5 on the approach to runway 16L.

### 2. What is the touchdown zone elevation for runway 16L? (FAA-H-8083-15)

The TDZE is 710 MSL.

### 3. What is the bearing and distance of the MAP from the FAF? (FAA-H-8083-15)

The MAP is 164°, 3.8 NM from FAF for the localizer approach, and approximately the same distance for the full ILS approach.

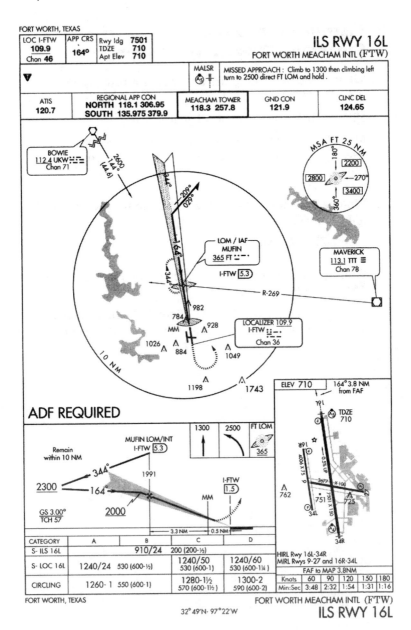

FORT WORTH, TEXAS

| LOC I-FTW<br>**109.9**<br>Chan **46** | APP CRS<br>**164°** | Rwy ldg **7501**<br>TDZE **710**<br>Apt Elev **710** | | **ILS RWY 16L**<br>FORT WORTH MEACHAM INTL (FTW) |
|---|---|---|---|---|

| | | MALSR<br>Ⓐ | MISSED APPROACH : Climb to 1300 then climbing left turn to 2500 direct FT LOM and hold . |

| ATIS<br>**120.7** | REGIONAL APP CON<br>**NORTH 118.1 306.95**<br>**SOUTH 135.975 379.9** | MEACHAM TOWER<br>**118.3 257.8** | GND CON<br>**121.9** | CLNC DEL<br>**124.65** |
|---|---|---|---|---|

**ADF REQUIRED**

| CATEGORY | A | B | C | D |
|---|---|---|---|---|
| S- ILS 16L | | 910/24 | 200 (200-½) | |
| S- LOC 16L | 1240/24 | 530 (600-½) | 1240/50<br>530 (600-1) | 1240/60<br>530 (600-1¼ ) |
| CIRCLING | 1260- 1 | 550 (600-1) | 1280-1½<br>570 (600-1½ ) | 1300-2<br>590 (600-2) |

HIRL Rwy 16L-34R
MIRL Rwys 9-27 and 16R-34L

FAF to MAP 3.8NM

| Knots | 60 | 90 | 120 | 150 | 180 |
|---|---|---|---|---|---|
| Min:Sec | 3:48 | 2:32 | 1:54 | 1:31 | 1:16 |

FORT WORTH, TEXAS

32°49'N- 97°22'W

FORT WORTH MEACHAM INTL (FTW)
**ILS RWY 16L**

# Additional Study Questions

1. What is the function of the "high" and "low" setting on the marker beacon receiver? (AFM)

2. Is capability to receive and identify marker beacons required for all ILS approach procedures? (14 CFR 91.175)

3. If RAIM is not available or becomes unavailable during a GPS approach procedure, what is the recommended procedure? (AIM 1-1-19)

4. Are the required visibility figures in the instrument minimums sections on approach charts statute or nautical? (FAA-H-8083-15)

5. The acronym LAHSO refers to what specific ATC procedure? (AIM 4-3-11)

6. What is a side-step maneuver? (FAA-H-8083-15)

7. Be capable of locating and defining the following approach chart abbreviations:

| | | | |
|------|-----------|------|---------|
| ALS | HIRL | MAP | SDF |
| ALSF | IAF | MDA | TAA |
| BC | IM | NA | TCH |
| DA | LDA | NoPT | TDZE |
| DH | LNAV/VNAV | OM | TDZL |
| FAF | LDIN | RCLS | VDP |
| GLS | LOM | RNP | WP/WPT |
| HAA | LR | RVR | |
| HAT | MALS | S | |

8. Define the term, "final approach point." (AIM Glossary)

# Practical Test Checklists

# Appendix 1

# Applicant's Practical Test Checklist

Appointment with Examiner _____

Examiner's Name _____

Location _____

Date/Time _____

## Acceptable Aircraft

### Aircraft Documents
___Airworthiness Certificate

___Registration Certificate

___Rating Limitations

### Aircraft Maintenance Records
___Logbook Record of Airworthiness Inspections and AD Compliance

___Pilot's Operating Handbook, FAA-Approved Airplane Flight Manual

___Current Weight and Balance Data

## Personal Equipment

___View-Limiting Device

___Current Aeronautical Charts

___Computer and Plotter

___Flight Plan Form

___Flight Logs

___Current AIM, Airport Facility Directory, and Appropriate Publications

## Personal Records

___Identification — Photo/Signature ID

___Pilot Certificate

___Current and Appropriate Medical Certificate

___Completed FAA Form 8710-1, Airman Certificate and/or
    Rating Application with Instructor's Signature (if applicable)

___Airman Knowledge Test Report

___Pilot Logbook with Appropriate Instructor Endorsements

___Notice of Disapproval (if applicable)

___Approved School Graduation Certificate (if applicable)

___Examiner's Fee (if applicable)

# Examiner's Practical Test Checklist

Applicant's Name _____

Location _____

Date/Time _____

## I. Preflight Preparation

____ A. Weather Information

____ B. Cross-Country Flight Planning

## II. Preflight Procedures

____ A. Aircraft Systems Related to IFR Operations

____ B. Aircraft Flight Instruments and Navigation Equipment

____ C. Instrument Cockpit Check

## III. Air Traffic Control Clearances and Procedures

____ A. Air Traffic Control Clearances

____ B. Compliance with Departure, En Route, and Arrival Procedures and Clearances

____ C. Holding Procedures

## IV. Flight By Reference to Instruments

____ A. Basic Instrument Flight Maneuvers

____ B. Recovery from Unusual Flight Attitudes

## V. Navigation Systems

____ Intercepting and Tracking Navigational Systems and DME Arcs

## VI. Instrument Approach Procedures

____ A. Nonprecision Approach (NPA)

____ B. Precision Approach (PA)

____ C. Missed Approach

____ D. Circling Approach

____ E. Landing from a Straight-in or Circling Approach

*Continued*

## VII. Emergency Operations

____ A. Loss of Communications

____ B. One Engine Inoperative During Straight-and-Level Flight and Turns (Multiengine Airplane)

____ C. One Engine Inoperative—Instrument Approach (Multiengine Airplane)

____ D. Loss of Primary Flight Instrument Indicators

## VIII. Postflight Procedures

____Checking Instruments and Equipment

# Certified Flight
# Instructor
# Supplement      Appendix 2

# Certified Flight Instructor–
# Instrument Airplane Supplement

This CFII appendix has been designed for use in conjunction with the material presented in Chapters 1–4 of this guide, for one comprehensive outline and reference. A review of this guide should provide the CFII applicant with aid for preparation and accomplishment of the Flight Instructor Instrument Airplane practical check. This appendix may be supplemented with other study materials as noted in parentheses after each question.

## A. Flight by Reference to Instruments

### 1. Define basic attitude instrument flying. (FAA-H-8083-15)

Attitude instrument flying may be defined as the control of an aircraft's spatial position by using instruments rather than outside visual references.

### 2. What are the two basic methods for learning attitude instrument flying? (FAA-H-8083-15)

The two basic methods used for learning attitude instrument flying are "control and performance" and "primary and supporting." Both methods involve the use of the same instruments, and both use the same responses for attitude control. They differ in their reliance on the attitude indicator and interpretation of other instruments.

### 3. Explain the control and performance method of attitude instrument flying. (FAA-H-8083-15)

Aircraft performance is achieved by controlling the aircraft attitude and power (angle of attack and thrust to drag relationship). Aircraft attitude is the relationship of its longitudinal and lateral axes to the Earth's horizon. An aircraft is flown in instrument flight by controlling the attitude and power, as necessary, to produce the desired performance. This is known as the control and performance method of attitude instrument flying and can be applied to any basic instrument maneuver. The three general categories of instruments are control, performance, and navigation instruments.

## 4. What are the control instruments? (FAA-H-8083-15)

The control instruments display immediate attitude and power indications and are calibrated to permit attitude and power adjustments in precise amounts. In this discussion, the term "power" is used in place of the more technically correct term "thrust or drag relationship." Control is determined by reference to the attitude indicator and power indicators. These power indicators vary with aircraft and may include tachometers, manifold pressure, engine pressure ratio, fuel flow, etc.

## 5. What are the performance instruments? (FAA-H-8083-15)

The performance instruments indicate the aircraft's actual performance. Performance is determined by reference to the altimeter, airspeed or Mach indicator, vertical speed indicator, heading indicator, angle-of-attack indicator, and turn-and-slip indicator.

## 6. What are the navigation instruments? (FAA-H-8083-15)

The navigation instruments indicate the position of the aircraft in relation to a selected navigation facility or fix. This group of instruments includes various types of course indicators, range indicators, glideslope indicators, and bearing pointers.

## 7. What are the procedural steps used in the control and performance method of attitude instrument flying? (FAA-H-8083-15)

*Establish* an attitude and power setting on the control instruments that will result in the desired performance. Known or computed attitude changes and approximate power settings will help to reduce the pilot's workload.

*Trim* until control pressures are neutralized. Trimming for hands-off flight is essential for smooth, precise aircraft control. It allows pilots to divert their attention to other cockpit duties with minimum deviation from the desired attitude.

*Cross-check* the performance instruments to determine if the established attitude or power setting is providing the desired performance. The cross-check involves both seeing and interpreting. If a deviation is noted, determine the magnitude and direction of adjustment required to achieve the desired performance.

*Adjust* the attitude or power setting on the control instruments as necessary.

## 8. How is attitude control accomplished? (FAA-H-8083-15)

Proper control of aircraft attitude is the result of maintaining a constant attitude, knowing when and how much to change the attitude, and smoothly changing the attitude a precise amount. Aircraft attitude control is accomplished by properly using the attitude indicator. The attitude reference provides an immediate, direct, and corresponding indication of any change in aircraft pitch or bank attitude.

## 9. How is pitch control accomplished? (FAA-H-8083-15)

Pitch changes are made by changing the "pitch attitude" of the miniature aircraft or fuselage dot by precise amounts in relation to the horizon. These changes are measured in degrees or fractions thereof, or bar widths depending upon the type of attitude reference. The amount of deviation from the desired performance will determine the magnitude of the correction.

## 10. How is bank control accomplished? (FAA-H-8083-15)

Bank changes are made by changing the "bank attitude" or bank pointers by precise amounts in relation to the bank scale. The bank scale is normally graduated at 0°, 10°, 20°, 30°, 60°, and 90° and may be located at the top or bottom of the attitude reference. Normally, use a bank angle that approximates the degrees to turn, not to exceed 30°.

## 11. How is power control accomplished? (FAA-H-8083-15)

Proper power control results from the ability to smoothly establish or maintain desired airspeeds in coordination with attitude changes. Power changes are made by throttle adjustments and reference to the power indicators. Power indicators are not affected by such factors as turbulence, improper trim, or inadvertent control pressures. Therefore, in most aircraft little attention is required to ensure the power setting remains constant. From experience in an aircraft, you know approximately how far to move the throttles to change the power a given amount. Therefore, you can make power changes primarily by throttle movement and then cross-check the indicators to establish a more precise setting. The key is to avoid fixating on the indicators while setting the power. A knowledge of approximate power settings for various flight configurations will help you avoid overcontrolling power.

12. **Explain the primary and supporting method of attitude instrument flying.** (FAA-H-8083-15)

For any maneuver or condition of flight, the pitch, bank, and power control requirements are most clearly indicated by certain key instruments. The instruments that provide the most pertinent and essential information will be referred to as primary instruments. Supporting instruments back up and supplement the information shown on the primary instruments.

13. **What instruments are used to determine and control pitch?** (FAA-H-8083-15)

Attitude indicator, altimeter, airspeed indicator, and vertical speed indicator.

14. **What instruments are used to determine and control bank?** (FAA-H-8083-15)

Attitude indicator, heading indicator, magnetic compass, and turn coordinator.

15. **What instruments are used to determine and control power?** (FAA-H-8083-15)

Airspeed indicator and engine instruments, which are the manifold pressure gauge (MP), tachometer/RPM, and for jets, engine pressure ratio (EPR).

16. **What are the three fundamental skills used in all instrument flight maneuvers?** (FAA-H-8083-15)

Instrument cross-check, instrument interpretation and aircraft control.

### 17. What does the first fundamental skill of instrument cross-checking consist of? (FAA-H-8083-15)

Cross-checking is the continuous and logical observation of instruments for attitude and performance information. In attitude instrument flying, the pilot maintains an attitude by reference to instruments that will produce the desired result in performance. Due to human error, instrument error, and airplane performance differences in various atmospheric and loading conditions, it is impossible to establish an attitude and have performance remain constant for a long period of time. These variables make it necessary for the pilot to constantly check the instruments and make appropriate changes in airplane attitude.

### 18. What are some of the common cross-check errors students make? (FAA-H-8083-15)

*Fixation* — staring at a single instrument; may be related to difficulties with one or both of the other fundamental skills. Student may be fixating because of uncertainty about reading the heading indicator (interpretation), or because of inconsistency in rolling out of turns (control).

*Omission* of an instrument from their cross-check; may be caused by failure to anticipate significant instrument indications following attitude changes.

*Emphasis* on a single instrument, instead of on the combination of instruments necessary for attitude information; student naturally tends to rely on the instrument they understand most readily, even when it provides erroneous or inadequate information. Reliance on a single instrument is poor technique.

### 19. What does the second fundamental skill of instrument interpretation consist of? (FAA-H-8083-15)

The second fundamental skill, instrument interpretation, requires the most thorough study and analysis. You must understand each instrument's construction and operating principles. Then you must apply this knowledge to the performance of the aircraft you are flying, the particular maneuvers to be executed, the cross-check and control techniques applicable to that aircraft, and the flight conditions in which you are operating.

### 20. What does the third fundamental skill of aircraft control consist of? (FAA-H-8083-15)

When you use instruments as substitutes for outside references, the necessary control responses and thought processes are the same as those for controlling aircraft performance by means of outside references. Knowing the desired attitude of the aircraft with respect to the natural and artificial horizon, you maintain the attitude or change it by moving the appropriate controls.

### 21. What are the four components of aircraft control? (FAA-H-8083-15)

*Pitch control*—controlling the rotation of the aircraft about the lateral axis by movement of the elevators. After interpreting the pitch attitude from the proper flight instruments, you exert control pressures to effect the desired pitch attitude with reference to the horizon.

*Bank control*—controlling the angle made by the wing and the horizon. After interpreting the bank attitude from the appropriate instruments, you exert the necessary pressures to move the ailerons and roll the aircraft about the longitudinal axis.

*Power control*—used when interpretation of the flight instruments indicates a need for a change in thrust.

*Trim*—used to relieve all control pressures held after a desired attitude has been attained. An improperly trimmed aircraft requires constant control pressures, produces tension, distracts your attention from cross-checking, and contributes to abrupt and erratic attitude control. The pressures you feel on the controls must be those you apply while controlling a planned change in aircraft attitude, not pressures held because you let the aircraft control you.

# B. Instrument Certification Regulations

1. **What conditions must exist for an instrument instructor, conducting a flight lesson, to log instrument time?** (14 CFR 61.51)

   An authorized instructor may log instrument flight time when conducting instrument flight instruction in actual instrument flight conditions.

2. **What time is considered "training" time and how should this be logged?** (14 CFR 61.51)

   a. A person may log training time when that person receives training from an authorized instructor in an aircraft, flight simulator, or flight training device.

   b. The training time must be logged in a logbook and must be endorsed in a legible manner by the authorized instructor; and include a description of the training given, the length of the training lesson, and the authorized instructor's signature, certificate number, and certificate expiration date.

3. **Concerning instructional flights with both an authorized flight instructor and a certified pilot on board, which person is allowed to log pilot-in-command time?** (14 CFR 61.51)

   Both the CFII and private pilot will log PIC time. Provided the private pilot is sole manipulator of the controls of an aircraft for which the pilot is rated, that pilot may log the time as PIC.

4. **For the purposes of meeting the recent instrument experience requirements, what information must be recorded in the person's logbook?** (14 CFR 61.51)

   a. The location and type of each instrument approach accomplished; and

   b. The name of the safety pilot, if required.

## 5. What does an instrument proficiency check consist of? (14 CFR 61.57)

An instrument proficiency check shall consist of a representative number of tasks required by the instrument rating practical test. A useful table has been included in the "Introduction" section of the Instrument Rating PTS, (FAA-S-8081-4)—a task table with "PC" as one of the columns. Conducting an IPC in accordance with this standard is a requirement.

## 6. Who can give an instrument proficiency check? (14 CFR 61.57)

14 CFR §61.57 states that the instrument proficiency check must be given by—

a. An examiner;

b. A person authorized by the U.S. Armed Forces to conduct instrument flight tests, provided the person being tested is a member of the U.S. Armed Forces;

c. A company check pilot who is authorized to conduct instrument flight tests under Part 121, 125, or 135, and provided that both the check pilot and the pilot being tested are employees of that operator;

d. An authorized instructor; or

e. A person approved by the Administrator to conduct instrument practical tests.

## 7. The instrument proficiency check required by 14 CFR §61.57 can be accomplished by flying with an authorized flight instructor. Does that CFI have to be a CFII? (14 CFR 61.193 and AC 61-98A)

If given by a CFI in a single-engine airplane, the CFI should hold an instrument airplane rating on his or her instructor certificate. If given in a multi-engine airplane, the CFI should hold both instrument airplane and airplane multi-engine ratings on his or her instructor certificate. A check in a helicopter should be given by a CFI holding an instrument helicopter rating on his or her instructor certificate. These prerequisites are necessary to conform to the requirements of 14 CFR §§61.193(a) and 61.195(b), and assure that the CFI has qualifications appropriate to the category and class of aircraft.

8. **Can the instrument proficiency check be given in a flight training device or flight simulator?** (AC 61-98A)

Part or all of the check may be conducted in a flight training device or flight simulator that meets the requirements of 14 CFR §141.41. The FAA FSDO having jurisdiction over the area where the device is used must specifically approve each flight training device or flight simulator. If planning to use a flight training device or flight simulator to conduct all or part of an instrument proficiency check, instructors should contact the local FSDO to verify the approval status of the device.

9. **What are several pre-check considerations a CFI should give thought to prior to conducting an IPC?** (AC 61-98A)

The CFI should structure an instrument proficiency check in a manner similar to that of the flight review, tailoring the check to the needs of the pilot, reaching mutual agreement on the scope of the check, and developing a plan for accomplishing it. The CFI and pilot should discuss the operating conditions under which the check will be conducted. If the check is conducted in an airplane, the check may be under VFR or IFR in simulated instrument conditions, or it may be under IFR in actual instrument conditions. If the check is conducted under IFR, whether conditions are simulated or actual, the CFI should ensure that the aircraft meets all Part 91 requirements for operating under IFR. Additionally, if the pilot receiving the check is no longer current under IFR, the CFI should be aware that he or she will be the pilot-in-command during the flight and must meet IFR currency requirements. The CFI should also discuss crewmember roles and responsibilities with the pilot.

10. **What standards shall be used to determine successful completion of the IPC?** (14 CFR 61.57)

When conducting an instrument proficiency check, the flight instructor should use the Instrument Rating PTS as the primary reference for specific maneuvers and any associated tolerances. A pilot taking an instrument proficiency check should be expected to meet the criteria of the specific tasks selected in this PTS.

## 11. What areas of knowledge should be reviewed by the CFI when conducting the knowledge portion of an IPC? (AC 61-98A)

The CFI should determine that the pilot has adequate knowledge and understanding of 14 CFR Part 91, especially Subpart B, "Instrument Flight Rules"; Subpart C, "Equipment, Instrument, and Certificate Requirements"; and Subpart E, "Maintenance, Preventive Maintenance, and Alterations." Additionally, the CFI should determine that the pilot has adequate knowledge and understanding of the following areas:

a. Instrument en route and approach chart interpretation, including Departure Procedures (DPs) and Standard Terminal Arrival Routes (STAR).

b. Obtaining and analyzing weather information, including knowledge of hazardous weather phenomena.

c. Preflight planning, including aircraft performance data, application of Notices to Airmen (NOTAM) information, fuel requirements, alternate requirements, and use of appropriate FAA publications such as the Airport/Facility Directory.

d. Aircraft systems related to IFR operations, including appropriate operating methods, limitations, and emergency procedures due to equipment failure.

e. Aircraft flight instruments and navigation equipment, including characteristics, limitations, operating techniques, and emergency procedures due to malfunction or failure, such as lost communications procedures.

f. Determining the airworthiness status of the aircraft for instrument flight, including required inspections and documents.

g. Air Traffic Control (ATC) procedures pertinent to flight under IFR with emphasis on elements of ATC clearances and pilot/controller responsibilities.

12. **After conducting the knowledge portion of an IPC, what actions should the CFI request the pilot to complete prior to conducting the flight skill portion of the check?** (AC 61-98A)

The CFI should ask the pilot to prepare for the skill portion of the proficiency check by completing the necessary flight planning, obtaining current weather data, filing a flight plan, and conducting the preflight inspection. In order to more fully evaluate the pilot's skills under normal operating conditions, the CFI may wish to have the pilot conduct a short IFR cross-country flight in conjunction with the rest of the proficiency check.

13. **What are some of the general considerations a CFI should have in determining the specific maneuvers and procedures for an IPC?** (14 CFR 61.57, AC 61-98A)

Specifically, an instrument proficiency check should consist of a representative number of tasks required by the Instrument Rating PTS. Generally, the maneuvers and procedures selected for the IPC should be comprehensive enough to enable the CFI to determine that the pilot can safely operate under IFR in a broad range of conditions appropriate to the aircraft flown and the ATC environment selected. Proper adherence to ATC clearances should be especially emphasized. Regardless of the maneuvers and procedures selected, the CFI should ensure that the pilot demonstrates satisfactory basic attitude instrument flying skills.

14. **What postflight actions and logbook entries should occur upon completion of an IPC?** (AC 61-98A)

Upon completion of the proficiency check, the CFI should complete the plan and checklist (if used) and debrief the pilot on the results of the check (satisfactory or unsatisfactory). Regardless of the determination, the CFI should provide the pilot with a comprehensive analysis of his or her performance, including suggestions for improving any weak areas. If the proficiency check was unsatisfactory, the CFI should not endorse the pilot's logbook, but should sign the logbook to record the instruction given. If the proficiency check was satisfactory, the endorsement for a satisfactory proficiency check should be in accordance with the current issue of AC 61-65. If a lesson plan and checklist was used, the CFI may wish to retain the plan as a record of the scope and content of the competency check, even though not required.

## 15. What are the general requirements for a person to be eligible for an instrument rating? (14 CFR 61.65)

a. Hold at least a current private pilot certificate with an airplane, helicopter, or powered-lift rating appropriate to the instrument rating sought;

b. Be able to read, speak, write, and understand the English language. If the applicant is unable to meet any of these requirements due to a medical condition, the Administrator may place such operating limitations on the applicant's pilot certificate as are necessary for the safe operation of the aircraft;

c. Receive and log ground training from an authorized instructor or accomplish a home-study course of training on the aeronautical knowledge areas that apply to the instrument rating sought;

d. Receive a logbook or training record endorsement from an authorized instructor certifying that the person is prepared to take the required knowledge test;

e. Receive and log training on the areas of operation from an authorized instructor in an aircraft, flight simulator, or flight training device that represents an airplane, helicopter, or powered-lift appropriate to the instrument rating sought;

f. Receive a logbook or training record endorsement from an authorized instructor certifying that the person is prepared to take the required practical test;

g. Pass the required knowledge test on the aeronautical knowledge; however, an applicant is not required to take another knowledge test when that person already holds an instrument rating; and

h. Pass the required practical test on the areas of operation in an airplane, helicopter, or powered-lift appropriate to the rating sought; or a flight simulator or a flight training device appropriate to the rating sought and for the specific maneuver or instrument approach procedure performed. If an approved flight training device is used for the practical test, the instrument approach procedures conducted in that flight training device are limited to one precision and one nonprecision approach, provided the flight training device is approved for the procedure performed.

## 16. What are the aeronautical knowledge requirements for a person to be eligible for an instrument rating? (14 CFR 61.65)

A person who applies for an instrument rating must have received and logged ground training from an authorized instructor or accomplished a home-study course on the following aeronautical knowledge areas that apply to the instrument rating sought:

a. Federal Aviation Regulations that apply to flight operations under IFR;

b. Appropriate information that applies to IFR operations in the *Aeronautical Information Manual*;

c. Air traffic control system and procedures for instrument flight operations;

d. IFR navigation and approaches by use of navigation systems;

e. Use of IFR en route and instrument approach procedure charts;

f. Procurement and use of aviation weather reports and forecasts and the elements of forecasting weather trends based on that information and personal observation of weather conditions;

g. Safe and efficient operation of aircraft under instrument flight rules and conditions;

h. Recognition of critical weather situations and windshear avoidance;

i. Aeronautical decision making and judgment; and

j. Crew resource management, including crew communication and coordination.

## 17. What are the flight proficiency requirements for a person to be eligible for an instrument rating? (14 CFR 61.65)

A person who applies for an instrument rating must receive and log training from an authorized instructor in an aircraft, or in a flight simulator or flight training device that includes the following areas of operation:

a. Preflight preparation;

b. Preflight procedures;

c. Air traffic control clearances and procedures;

d. Flight by reference to instruments;

e. Navigation systems;

f. Instrument approach procedures;

g. Emergency operations; and

h. Postflight procedures.

## 18. What are the aeronautical experience requirements for a person to be eligible for an instrument rating? (14 CFR 61.65)

A person who applies for an instrument rating must have logged the following:

a. At least 50 hours of cross-country flight time as pilot-in-command, of which at least 10 hours must be in airplanes for an instrument-airplane rating; and

b. A total of 40 hours of actual or simulated instrument time on the areas of operation, to include—

- At least 15 hours of instrument flight training from an authorized instructor in the aircraft category for which the instrument rating is sought;

- At least 3 hours of instrument training that is appropriate to the instrument rating sought from an authorized instructor in preparation for the practical test within the 60 days preceding the date of the test;

- For an instrument-airplane rating, instrument training on cross-country flight procedures specific to airplanes that includes at least one cross-country flight in an airplane performed under IFR, and consists of—
  - A distance of at least 250 NM along airways or ATC-directed routing;
  - An instrument approach at each airport; and
  - Three different kinds of approaches with the use of navigation systems.

## 19. What regulations apply if flight simulators or flight training devices are used for some of the training required for the instrument rating? (14 CFR 61.65 and AC 61-126)

If the instrument training was provided by an authorized instructor in a flight simulator or flight training device—

a. A maximum of 30 hours may be performed in that flight simulator or flight training device if the training was accomplished in accordance with 14 CFR Part 142, or

b. A maximum of 20 hours may be performed in that flight simulator or flight training device if the training was not accomplished in accordance with 14 CFR Part 142.

c. A maximum of 10 hours of the total flight simulator or flight training device time may be performed in a personal computer-based aviation training device (PCATD).

## 20. What is the minimum length of time a flight instructor is required to retain a record of their flight instruction activity? (14 CFR 61.189)

Each flight instructor must retain the records required by 14 CFR Part 61 for at least 3 years.

### 21. What are the required records a flight instructor must retain? (14 CFR 61.189)

A flight instructor must maintain a record in a logbook or a separate document that contains the following:

a. The name of each person whose logbook or student pilot certificate that instructor has endorsed for solo flight privileges, and the date of the endorsement; and

b. The name of each person that instructor has endorsed for a knowledge test or practical test, and the record shall also indicate the kind of test, the date, and the results.

### 22. What qualifications must a flight instructor possess before instruction may be given for the issuance of an instrument rating? (14 CFR 61.195)

A flight instructor who provides instrument flight training for the issuance of an instrument rating or a type rating not limited to VFR must hold an instrument rating on his or her flight instructor certificate and pilot certificate that is appropriate to the category and class of aircraft in which instrument training is being provided.

### 23. Can a CFII give instrument instruction in a multi-engine airplane if the instructor does not possess a multi-engine instructor rating or a multi-engine rating on his/her pilot certificate? (14 CFR 61.195)

No. A flight instructor who provides instrument flight training for the issuance of an instrument rating or a type rating not limited to VFR must hold an instrument rating on his or her flight instructor certificate and pilot certificate that is appropriate to the category and class of aircraft in which instrument training is being provided.

# C. Logbook Entries Related to Instrument Certification

1. **What advisory circular contains recommended sample endorsements for use by authorized instructors when endorsing airmen pilot logbooks?** (AC 61-65E)

   AC 61-65E—*Certification: Pilots and Flight and Ground Instructors*

2. **Each instructor endorsement should include what information?** (AC 61-65E)

   Each endorsement should include—

   a. Instructor signature
   b. Date of signature
   c. CFI certificate number
   d. Certificate expiration date

3. **Give examples of the endorsements you would use when endorsing a logbook for a pilot applying for an instrument rating.** (AC 61-65E)

   **Aeronautical knowledge test: §§61.35(a)(1) and 61.65(a), (b)**
   I certify that (First name, MI, Last name) has received the required training of §61.65(b). I have determined that he/she is prepared for the (name the knowledge test).

   /s/     [date]     J.J. Jones     987654321CFI     Exp. 12-31-05

   **Flight proficiency/practical test: §61.65(a)(6)**
   I certify that (First name, MI, Last name) has received the required training of §61.65(c) and (d). I have determined he/she is prepared for the Instrument—(Airplane, Helicopter, or Powered-lift) practical test.

   /s/     [date]     J. J. Jones     987654321CFI     Exp. 12-31-05

4. **Give an example of the endorsement you would use for a pilot who has just completed an instrument proficiency check.** (AC 61-65E)

I certify that (First name, MI, Last name), (pilot certificate), (certificate number), has satisfactorily completed the instrument proficiency check of §61.57(d) in a (list make and model of aircraft) on (date).

/s/    [date]    J. J. Jones    987654321CFI    Exp. 12-31-05

# D. Fundamentals of Instructing

## 1. Briefly define the term "learning." (FAA-H-8083-9)

Learning can be defined as a change in behavior as a result of experience.

## 2. What are the basic characteristics of learning? (FAA-H-8083-9)

*Learning is purposeful* —Each student is a unique individual whose past experience affects readiness to learn and understanding of the requirements involved.

*Learning comes through experience*—Learning is an individual process. Knowledge cannot be poured into the student's head. The student can learn only from individual experience.

*Learning is multifaceted* —The learning process may include verbal elements, conceptual elements, perceptual elements, emotional elements, and elements of problem solving, all taking place at once.

*Learning is an active process*—For students to learn, they must react and respond.

## 3. What are the laws of learning? (FAA-H-8083-9)

These are rules and principles that generally apply to the learning process. The first three are the basic laws; the last three laws are the result of experimental studies.

*The law of readiness* —individuals learn best when they are ready to learn, and they do not learn if they see no reason for learning.

*The law of exercise*—those things most often repeated are best remembered. It is the basis of practice and drill.

*The law of effect*—learning is strengthened when accompanied by a pleasant or satisfying feeling, and that learning is weakened when associated with an unpleasant feeling.

*The law of primacy*—the state of being first, often creates a strong, almost unshakable, impression. What is taught must be right the first time.

*The law of intensity*—a vivid, dramatic, or exciting learning experience teaches more than a routine or boring experience.

*The law of recency*—the things most recently learned are best remembered.

## 4. How do people learn? (FAA-H-8083-9)

All learning involves the following:

*Perception* —Initially all learning comes from perceptions that are directed to the brain by one or more of the five senses (sight, hearing, touch, smell and taste).

*Insight*—The grouping of perceptions into meaningful wholes.

*Motivation*—The most dominant force governing the student's progress and ability to learn.

### 5. What are the four levels of learning? (FAA-H-8083-9)

*Rote learning* — The ability to repeat back something that one has been taught, without understanding or being able to apply what has been learned.

*Understanding* — What has been taught.

*Application* — Achieving the skill to apply what has been learned and to perform correctly.

*Correlation* — Associating and correlating what has been learned with other things previously learned or encountered.

### 6. Why do individuals forget what has been learned? (FAA-H-8083-9)

*Disuse* — A person forgets these things which are not used.

*Interference* — People forget a thing because a certain experience has overshadowed it, or the learning of similar things has interfered.

*Repression* — Forgetting is due to the submersion of ideas into the unconscious mind. Material that is unpleasant or produces anxiety may be treated this way by individuals, but not intentionally.

### 7. What actions can the instructor take to assist individuals in remembering what has been learned? (FAA-H-8083-9)

*Praise* stimulates remembering; responses that give a pleasurable return tend to be repeated.

*Recall* is prompted by association. Each bit of information or action that is associated with something to be learned tends to facilitate its later recall by the student.

*Favorable attitudes* aid retention; people learn and remember only what they wish to know. Without motivation there is little chance for recall.

*Learning* with all our senses is most effective. Although we generally receive what we learn through the eyes and ears, other senses also contribute to most perceptions.

*Meaningful repetition* aids recall; each repetition gives the student an opportunity to gain a clearer and more accurate perception of the subject to be learned, but mere repetition does not guarantee retention.

### 8. What are "defense mechanisms"? (FAA-H-8083-9)

Certain behavior patterns are called defense mechanisms because they are subconscious defenses against the realities of unpleasant situations.

### 9. What are several common defense mechanisms? (FAA-H-8083-9)

*Repression*—a person places uncomfortable thoughts into inaccessible areas of the unconscious mind.

*Denial*—a refusal to accept external reality because it is too threatening.

*Compensation*—a process of psychologically counterbalancing perceived weaknesses by emphasizing strength in other areas.

*Projection*—an individual places his or her own unacceptable impulses onto someone else.

*Rationalization*—a subconscious technique for justifying actions that otherwise would be unacceptable.

*Reaction formation*—a person fakes a belief opposite to the true belief because the true belief causes anxiety.

*Fantasy*—occurs when a student engages in daydreams about how things should be rather than doing anything about how things are.

*Displacement*—results in an unconscious shift of emotion, affect, or desire from the original object to a more acceptable, less threatening substitute.

### 10. What rules should an instructor follow to ensure good human relations with the student? (FAA-H-8083-9)

a. Keep students motivated

b. Keep students informed

c. Approach students as individuals

d. Give credit when due

e. Criticize constructively

f. Be consistent

g. Admit errors

## 11. What are the basic steps involved in the teaching process? (FAA-H-8083-9)

The teaching of new material can be broken down into the steps of:

a. Preparation

b. Presentation

c. Application

d. Review and evaluation

## 12. What are the three most common teaching methods? (FAA-H-8083-9)

a. Lecture method

b. Guided discussion method

c. Demonstration/performance method

## 13. Discuss the "lecture" method of teaching. (FAA-H-8083-9)

The lecture is used primarily to introduce students to a new subject, but it is also a valuable method for summarizing ideas, showing relationships between theory and practice, and re-emphasizing main points.

## 14. What is the "guided discussion" method of teaching? (FAA-H-8083-9)

In contrast to the lecture method, where the instructor provides information, the guided discussion method relies on the students to provide ideas, experiences, opinions, and information. Through the skillful use of "lead-off" type questions, the instructor "draws out" what the student knows, rather than spending the class period telling them.

## 15. What is the "demonstration/performance" method of teaching? (FAA-H-8083-9)

This method of teaching is based on the simple, yet sound principle that we learn by doing.

16. **What are the five essential phases of the demonstration/ performance method of teaching?** (FAA-H-8083-9)

    a. Explanation

    b. Demonstration

    c. Student performance

    d. Instructor supervision

    e. Evaluation

17. **What are the three main steps involved when organizing the material for a particular lesson?** (FAA-H-8083-9)

    a. Introduction

    b. Development

    c. Conclusion

18. **The "introduction" step should contain which basic elements?** (FAA-H-8083-9)

    *Attention* — gain the student's attention and focus it on the subject involved.

    *Motivation* — should appeal to each student personally and accentuate his or her desire to learn.

    *Overview* — tells the student what is to be covered; a clear concise presentation of the objectives and key ideas; provides a road map of the route to be followed.

19. **Discuss the "development" step of a presentation.** (FAA-H-8083-9)

    This is the main part of the lesson. The instructor develops the subject matter in a manner that helps the student achieve desired learning outcomes. The instructor must logically organize the material to show the relationships of the main points.

20. **Define the term "integrated flight instruction."** (FAA-H-8083-9)

    Integrated flight instruction is flight instruction during which students are taught to perform flight maneuvers both by outside references and by reference to flight instruments, from the first time each maneuver is introduced.

## 21. What are the characteristics of an effective critique? (FAA-H-8083-9)

A critique should be:

*Objective* — An effective critique is focused on student performance and should not reflect the personal opinions, likes, dislikes, and biases of the instructor.

*Flexible* — An instructor must fit the tone, technique, and content of the critique to the occasion and the student.

*Acceptable* — Before students willingly accept their instructor's criticism, they must first accept the instructor. Effective critiques are presented with authority, conviction, sincerity, and from a position of recognizable competence.

*Comprehensive* — Effective critiques will cover a few major points or a few minor points as well as cover the overall strengths and weaknesses of the student.

*Constructive* — The instructor should provide positive guidance for correcting the faults and strengthening the weaknesses.

*Well organized* — Unless a critique follows some pattern of organization, a series of valid comments may lose their impact.

*Thoughtful* — An instructor should always be thoughtful towards the student's need for self-esteem, recognition, and approval from others.

*Specific* — The instructor's comments and recommendations should be specific, not so general that the student can find nothing to hold on to.

## 22. Control of human behavior involves understanding human needs. Name the six basic needs. (FAA-H-8083-9)

a. Physiological

b. Security

c. Belonging

d. Esteem

e. Cognitive and Aesthetic

f. Self-Actualization

### 23. What are the basic steps in planning a course of learning? (FAA-H-8083-9)

Before any important instruction can begin, the following must be considered:

a. Determination of standards and objectives.

b. Development and assembly of blocks of learning.

c. Identification of the blocks of learning.

### 24. What is a training syllabus? (FAA-H-8083-9)

A training syllabus is an outline of the course of training. It uses a step-by-step, building block progression of learning, with provisions for regular review and evaluations at prescribed stages of learning. The syllabus defines the unit of training, states objectives as to what the student is expected to accomplish during the unit, shows an organized plan for instruction, and dictates the evaluation process for either the unit or stages of learning.

### 25. What is a lesson plan? (FAA-H-8083-9)

A lesson plan is an organized outline or "blueprint" for a single instructional period and should be prepared in written form for each ground school and flight period. It should—

a. Tell what to do

b. What order to do it in

c. What procedure to use in teaching it

### 26. What items will a lesson plan always contain? (FAA-H-8083-9)

a. Lesson objective

b. Elements included

c. Schedule

d. Equipment

e. Instructor's actions

f. Student's actions

g. Completion standards

# E. Preflight Lesson on a Maneuver to be Performed In Flight

An FAA examiner will determine that the applicant exhibits instructional knowledge of the elements related to the planning of instructional activity. This will be accomplished by requiring the applicant to develop a lesson plan for any one of the required maneuvers. The following is an example of a lesson plan for a 90-minute instructional flight period.

Date _____

Lesson _____

Straight-and-Level Flight by Student _____

## Reference to Instruments

### Objective

To determine that the pilot:

1. Exhibits adequate knowledge of the elements related to attitude instrument flying during straight-and-level flight.

2. Maintains straight-and-level flight in the configuration specified by the examiner.

3. Maintains the heading within 10 degrees, altitude within 100 feet (30 meters), and airspeed within 10 knots.

4. Uses proper instrument cross check and interpretation, and applies the appropriate pitch, bank, power, and trim corrections.

### Elements

1. Instrument cross-check
2. Instrument interpretation
3. Aircraft control (pitch, bank, power, and trim)

### Schedule

1. Preflight—discuss lesson objective    :20
2. Inflight instructor demonstration    :20
3. Inflight student practice    :25
4. Postflight critique    :15
5. Assignment next lesson    :10

## Equipment

1. Instrument panel mockup
2. Chalkboard/notebook
3. View limiting device
4. *Instrument Flying Handbook*

## Instructor's Actions

1. Discuss lesson objective
2. Discuss concept of attitude instrument flying
3. Present straight-and-level flight on mockup from standpoint of pitch, bank, power, and trim
4. Inflight — Demonstrate straight-and-level flight by reference to instruments
5. Inflight — Direct student practice of straight-and-level flight by reference to instruments
6. Postflight — Critique student performance
7. Make reading assignments for next lesson

## Student's Actions

1. Discuss lesson objective
2. Listen, take notes, ask pertinent questions
3. Inflight — Observe instructor demonstration of straight-and-level flight by reference to instruments
4. Inflight — Practice of straight-and-level flight by reference to instruments
5. Postflight — Ask appropriate questions
6. Obtain reading assignments for next lesson

## Completion

The student should demonstrate that they have an understanding of the concept of attitude instrument flying and of the performance of straight-and-level flight by reference to instruments.

## Common Errors

1. Slow or improper cross-check during straight-and-level flight
2. Improper power control
3. Failure to make smooth, precise corrections, as required
4. Uncoordinated use of controls
5. Improper trim control

**Appendix 2**

# FAA Instrument Proficiency Check Guidance

# Appendix 3

The following is an excerpt from the FAA's Instrument Proficiency Check (IPC) Guidance document found at **www.faasafety.gov**. Visit **www.asa2fly.com/reader/oegi** to download the complete document, which includes additional information and helpful worksheets for both the CFII and IPC applicant.

**Appendix 3**

# Instrument Proficiency Check Guidance

## Introduction

The certificated flight instructor (CFI) performs one of the most vital and influential roles in aviation, because the aviation educator's work matters not just for the individual pilot, but for every passenger who entrusts his or her life to that pilot's knowledge, skill, and judgment.

The instrument flight instructor—the so-called "double-eye"—carries an even greater responsibility. Weather is still the factor most likely to result in aviation accidents with fatalities. Notwithstanding the common reminder that the instrument rating is not an "all weather license," the CFI-I's endorsement for instrument privileges attests that the pilot has the knowledge and skill to operate safely in instrument meteorological conditions (IMC) during all phases of flight.

Two special challenges arise for the CFI-I who administers the instrument proficiency check (IPC) described in 14 CFR §61.57(d). The CFI-I who trains a pilot for the initial instrument rating can develop a comprehensive picture of that pilot's instrument flying knowledge, skills, and judgment, usually in an aircraft familiar to both the CFI-I and the trainee. By contrast, an IPC more often requires short-term evaluation of an unknown pilot, possibly with the added challenge of an unfamiliar aircraft and/or avionics, particularly in technically advanced aircraft. In addition, the IPC is not always conducted in the "real-world" IMC flying environment.

To ensure that the IPC serves the purpose for which it was intended, the current version of the Practical Test Standards (PTS) for the instrument rating (FAA-S-8081-4D effective October 1, 2004) stipulates that the flight portion of an IPC must include certain aeronautical tasks specific to instrument flying. This guide offers additional (optional) guidance, with special emphasis on conducting a thorough ground review and on administering IPCs in aircraft with advanced avionics. The goal is to help the CFI-I determine that a pilot seeking an IPC endorsement has both the knowledge and skills for safe operation in all aspects of instrument flying.

# Step 1: Preparation

*Expectations:* Regulations for the flight review (14 CFR §61.56) require a minimum of one hour of ground training and one hour of flight training. While 14 CFR §61.57(d) does not stipulate a minimum time requirement for the IPC, a good rule of thumb is to plan at least 90 minutes of ground time and at least two hours of flight time for a solid evaluation of the pilot's instrument flying knowledge and skills. Depending on the pilot's level of instrument experience and currency, you may want to plan on two or more separate sessions to complete an IPC. For pilots with little or no recent instrument flying experience, it is a good idea to schedule an initial session in an appropriate aircraft training device (ATD).

*Regulatory Review:* The regulations (14 CFR §61.57(d)) state that an IPC must include "a representative number of tasks required by the instrument rating practical test." A thorough IPC should cover general operating and flight rules for IFR as set out in 14 CFR Part 91 and in the *Aeronautical Information Manual* (AIM). To make the best use of ground time, ask the pilot to review the *Instrument Procedures Handbook* (FAA-H-8261-1A), *Instrument Flying Handbook* (FAA-H-8083-15), and *Aviation Weather* and *Weather Services* in advance of your session. Remind the pilot to bring current copies of documents such as the instrument rating PTS, FAR/AIM, charts (en route and instrument approach procedures), Airport/Facility Directory (A/FD), and Pilot's Operating Handbook (POH) or Airplane Flight Manual (AFM) for the aircraft to be used.

As part of the IPC preparation process, you may want to ask the pilot to complete the IPC Prep Course available in the Aviation Learning Center at **www.faasafety.gov**. This online course lets the pilot review material at his or her own pace and focus attention on areas of particular interest.

*Cross-Country Flight Plan Assignment:* Because IFR flying is almost always for transportation purposes, structuring the IPC as an IFR cross-country—ideally one representative of the pilot's typical IFR flying—is an excellent way to evaluate real world instrument flying skills. The airport(s) to be used should have published instrument approach procedures. The flight plan should include consideration of all preflight planning elements required by 14 CFR §91.103, as well as appropriate instrument departure, arrival, and approach procedures. It should be based on a standard weather briefing for the day of the discussion and flight. If the ground and flight portions take place on different days, the pilot should have current weather for each session.

To ensure a thorough evaluation of the pilot's weather interpretation and analysis skills—especially if the weather for the actual IPC is MVFR or better—your own advance preparation might include obtaining a weather briefing for the assigned route on an IFR or low IFR (LIFR) day. You can either provide this IFR briefing to the pilot for advance analysis, or present it during the session for an on-the-spot review and evaluation.

# Step 2: Ground Review

Knowledge is key to safe instrument operation, but it needs to be much deeper than the ability to recite rules and regulations. Scenario-based training is a very effective way to test a pilot's knowledge in the context of real-world IFR flying, so consider using the pre-assigned XC flight plan as a basis for both the ground review and the actual flight. A good ground review technique is to work through rules and "real world" procedures related to each phase of flight from departure to the destination airport. Topics to cover include the following:

### Preflight (14 CFR §91.103)

For a flight under IFR, the pilot must become familiar with "all available information." For the pre-assigned flight plan, the pilot should be able to address the following topics:

### Weather (standard briefing)

- **Describe** weather for departure, en route, and arrival, to include discussion of forecast convective activity or freezing levels/cloud bases along the intended route. For example: "Conditions for departure are VFR, but we will encounter MVFR and IFR conditions en route. Conditions for ETA at destination are IFR. There is no convective activity in the forecast, but the freezing level is expected to be just above the filed altitude."
- **Evaluate** current/forecast weather in terms of:
  - Personal minimums
  - Aircraft equipment
  - Terrain/obstacle avoidance
  - Distance, time, and fuel to nearest VFR conditions

## Expected performance and equipment required (airworthiness)

- **Determine** that aircraft is appropriately equipped for proposed flight (14 CFR §§91.205(d), 91.171, Kinds of Operations Equipment List (KOEL) if provided in the Aircraft Flight Manual (AFM)).
- **Calculate** expected aircraft performance (takeoff/landing distances and cruise performance) under known and forecast conditions.
- **Describe** operation and failure modes of installed equipment (e.g., GPS, autopilot, avionics), and appropriate pilot response (including the requirement to report failures to ATC).

## Alternatives

- **Determine** if weather requires filing an alternate and, if so:
- **Designate** alternates that are not only "legal," but also appropriate to conditions, pilot experience, needs, etc. If planning to fly a GPS approach to the destination, consider the need to have a non-GPS approach at the alternate unless there is a WAAS-capable GPS. Can the pilot identify viable alternatives for every 25–30 nm along the route? Does he or she establish "tripwire" conditions related to personal minimums as triggers for diversion?

## Length/lighting of runways to be used

- **Determine** that available runway length is at least 150% of values shown in the POH/AFM, or at least 200% of the POH/AFM numbers for a wet, icy, or otherwise contaminated runway.
- **Explain** LAHSO procedures (AIM 4-3-11), if in effect at the airport(s) to be used.
- **Describe** expected lighting, including lighting as it applies to descent below MDA or DA (14 CFR §91.175).

## Traffic delays

- **Determine** whether traffic delays might require holding, and
- **Describe** holding procedures (AIM 5-3-7). During this part of the review, you may want to give the pilot a practice holding clearance and have him or her explain how the entry would be made from the en route heading to the holding fix. For aircraft equipped with GPS moving map navigators, does the pilot understand how to set up and use this equipment to fly a non-published ("random") holding pattern?

## How much fuel is required

- **Calculate** fuel requirements sufficient to fly approaches at both the destination and alternate, and
- **Decide** on the amount of reserve fuel (e.g., legal reserve plus safety margin appropriate to reported and forecast weather conditions).

## Risk Management and Personal Minimums

The ground discussion should include all risk factors that affect the planned flight, as well as the types of trips the pilot typically flies. The PAVE checklist is one way to make a structured identification and analysis. For example:

**P**ilot: general health, physical/mental/emotional state; proficiency, currency

**A**ircraft: airworthiness, equipment, performance capability

en**V**ironment: weather hazards, terrain, airports/runways to be used, conditions

**E**xternal pressures: meetings, people waiting at destination, etc.

For each risk factor identified, ask the pilot what strategies can be used to mitigate or eliminate the hazards. This part of the IPC also offers an excellent opportunity to discuss personal minimums, and to help the pilot complete a personal minimums worksheet if he or she has never done so.

*Personal Minimums Checklist:* One of the most important concepts to convey is that safe pilots understand the difference between what is "legal" in terms of the regulations, and what is "smart" or "safe" in terms of pilot experience and proficiency. For this reason, assistance in completing a Personal Minimums Checklist tailored to the pilot's individual circumstances is perhaps the single most important "take-away" item you can offer. Use the Personal Minimums Development Worksheet in Appendix 3 to help the pilot work through some of the questions that should be considered in establishing "hard" personal minimums, as well as in preflight and in-flight decision-making for flight under IFR.

It may also be helpful to include key findings from accident data. For example, instrument pilots should be aware that non-precision approaches have an accident rate five times greater than precision approaches. Circling approaches, particularly at night, also increase risk, so the pilot should consider such factors as how much of a tailwind can be acceptable in lieu of a circling approach.

## Taxi, Takeoff and Departure

Even at a familiar airport, departure under instrument meteorological conditions can be challenging. Topics to cover in this part of the review include:

### Taxi Procedures and Runway Incursion Avoidance

One of the FAA's top priorities is to reduce the frequency of runway incursions and the risk of a runway collision, so be sure that the pilot can correctly identify airport markings. Give the pilot a practice taxi clearance from ramp to runway, and ask him or her to show you on the airport diagram how to execute it. If the airports to be used have only a single runway, give the pilot taxi instructions for a more complex airport.

The FAA's Runway Safety Office (**http://www.faa.gov/runwaysafety/**) offers links to a number of resources available to help pilots operate safely on the airport surface. Sections 4-3-18 and 4-3-19 of the *Aeronautical Information Manual* (AIM) also offer guidance on safe taxi procedures, including taxi during low-visibility conditions.

### Instrument Departures (AIM 5-2-8)

All departure procedures (DPs) provide a way to depart the airport and transition safely to the en route structure, but proficient instrument pilots need to understand the difference between obstacle departure procedures (ODPs) and standard instrument departure procedures (SIDs). If the airport to be used has a SID, ask the pilot to explain how he or she would file and fly that specific procedure. Other questions to ask:

*Obstacle Departure Procedures:*

- What is an ODP, and where do you find it?
- What functions does the ODP serve?
- Do you need an ATC clearance to fly an ODP?
- Can ATC assign an ODP for departure from a non-towered airport?
- When should you fly an ODP?
- When departing from an airport without an ODP or SID, how will you ensure terrain/obstacle clearance until reaching a published MEA?

*Standard Instrument Departure Procedures:*

- What is a SID, and where do you find it?
- What functions does the SID serve?
- Can you fly a SID without ATC clearance?
- How do you file a SID (e.g., how is it stated in the flight plan)?

## En Route

Topics to review in connection with en route IFR operations include the following:

## Airways and Route Systems

Using the proposed route of flight on the appropriate IFR en route chart, ask the pilot to talk you through the journey. Be sure that the pilot is familiar with standard terms and symbols (e.g., MEA, MOCA, MORA, COP). Most pilots are familiar with the airway system de-fined by VOR facilities, but if your client flies with area navigation (RNAV) equipment, be sure to review the material in AIM 5-3-4 and AIM 5-1-8(d) on RNAV routes. Questions to ask:

- What is a published RNAV (Q) route, and who can use it?
- What is an "unpublished" RNAV route, and when can you fly it?
- What is the Magnetic Reference Bearing (MRB), and what are the limitations on its use?

## En Route Navigation (AIM 1-1-19)

This portion of the ground review should focus on use of the specific navigational equipment installed in the aircraft to be used for the IPC. For IPCs in aircraft equipped with GPS moving map navigators, special emphasis topics include:

- What requirements must your GPS meet before you can use it for IFR (e.g., equipment/installation approvals; operation in accordance with approved AFM or flight manual supplement, etc.).
- Under what conditions can you use GPS in place of ADF or DME equipment?
- Under what circumstances must you have (and use) means of naviga-tion other than GPS?
- What is RAIM, and when is it required?
- What are GPS NOTAMs (1-1-19), and how do you find them?

- Must your database be current?
- How and where are GPS database updates logged?
- How does course and distance information on a GPS navigation display differ from data presented on navigational charts and conventional instrumentation?

## En Route Weather

Since weather is at the heart of IFR flying, no IPC ground review can be complete without ensuring that the pilot is thoroughly familiar with sources of inflight weather information. A competent instrument pilot should know how to contact, address, and use the En Route Flight Advisory Service. As described in AIM 7-1-5, EFAS, or "Flight Watch," is a service specifically designed to provide timely, meaningful, and pertinent weather, as well as to collect and distribute pilot reports (PIREPs). EFAS is available on 122.0 between 5,000 MSL and 17,500 MSL; frequencies for other altitudes are listed in the AIM. Pilots should also be familiar with AIM 7-1-14 on ATC Inflight Weather Avoidance Assistance, including ATC descriptive terminology for convective activity and weather radar echoes. Be sure to note that there have been recent changes to the terminology that ATC uses to describe weather radar echoes.

Whether via approved installation or a portable handheld unit, weather datalink (AIM 7-1-11) provides both textual and graphical information that can help improve pilot situational awareness. While datalink has significant potential to improve GA safety, realization of these safety benefits depends heavily upon the pilot's understanding of the specific system's capabilities and limitations. With datalink, IFR pilots should pay particular attention to such system limitations as:

- *Latency.* Where would you find the time stamp or "valid until" time on the particular datalink weather information displayed in the cockpit? (*Note:* since initial processing and transmission of NEXRAD data can take several minutes, pilots should assume that datalink weather information will always be a minimum of seven to eight minutes older than shown on the time stamp and use datalink weather radar images for broad strategic avoidance of adverse weather.)

- *Coverage.* What coverage limitations are associated with the type of datalink network being used? (For example, ground-based systems that require a line-of-sight may have relatively limited coverage below 5,000 feet AGL. Satellite-based datalink weather systems can have limitations stemming from whether the network is in geosynchronous orbit or low earth orbit (LEO). Also, National Weather Service coverage has numerous gaps, especially in the western states.)

- *Content/format.* Since service providers often refine or enhance datalink products for cockpit display, pilots must be familiar with the content, format, and meaning of symbols and displays in the specific system.

## Abnormal Procedures and Emergencies

An IPC ground review of abnormal/emergency procedures for IFR operations should include the following topics:

- *Loss of two-way radio communications* (AIM 6-4-1): As stated in the AIM, a pilot who experiences a radio communications failure in VFR conditions should remain VFR and land as soon as practicable. In IFR conditions, the pilot should continue via the route assigned, vectored, expected, filed and at the highest of the following altitudes or flight levels for the route segment being flown: MEA, assigned, expected. Be sure to review the AIM guidance on clearance limits.

- *Loss of avionics/equipment* (AIM 5-3-3; 14 CFR §§91.185, 91.187): Any loss of navigational capability (e.g., loss of one VOR in a dual VOR installation) during operations in controlled airspace should be reported to ATC, along with information on the degree to which the problem affects the aircraft's ability to operate under IFR in the ATC system.

- *Loss of PFD/MFD/Autopilot:* Many pilots today operate with the situational awareness advantage of moving map navigators, "glass cockpit" avionics, and capable autopilots. If your client uses such equipment, or if it is installed in the aircraft to be used for the IPC, have the pilot describe failure modes and recommended procedures for each piece of equipment. The pilot should also be able to describe how one failure may affect other installed components (e.g., how would failure of the AHRS or ADC affect the autopilot?).

## Arrival and Approach Procedures

Check for the pilot's understanding of the ways to fly an instrument approach:

- Via pilot navigation ("own nav"):
  - Where are the IAFs?
  - Which IAFs require a course reversal, and how should it be flown?
- Via vectors
  - What are minimum vectoring altitudes?
  - How can you maintain position awareness relative to nearby terrain?
- Via direct to IF (intermediate fix)
  - Is a course reversal required if a racetrack is depicted at the IF?
  - What are the requirements for a controller to issue a clearance direct to the IF?

## Standard Terminal Arrival Procedures (AIM 5-4-1)

In reviewing the basics of flying a standard terminal arrival procedure (STAR), points to cover include the following:

- How do you file a STAR?
- When navigating a STAR, when may you descend?
- What does it mean if ATC instructs you to "descend via" the STAR?
- Do you need the approved chart in order to fly a STAR?
- What is an RNAV STAR?

## Terminal Arrival Areas (AIM 5-4-5)

Some pilots may not be familiar with the concept of terminal arrival areas, which have been designed to provide a seamless transition from the en route structure to the terminal environment for aircraft equipped with GPS or Flight Management System (FMS) navigational equipment. Questions to ask:

- How are TAA lateral boundaries identified?
- How can the pilot determine which area of the TAA the aircraft will enter?
- When ATC clears you to enter the TAA, what are you expected to do?

## Instrument Approach Procedures (AIM 5-4-5)

In addition to reviewing the terms, symbols, and basic steps for flying a conventional instrument approach procedure (e.g., ILS, LOC, VOR, NDB), you will also want to see whether the pilot understands RNAV (GPS) procedures and charting formats, with special emphasis on the minimums section. For example:

- What is LPV?
    - How do you know if you can fly to LPV minimums?
    - Does it include a DA or MDA?
    - At what point does the missed approach begin?
- What is LNAV/VNAV?
    - How do you know if you can fly to LNAV/VNAV minimums?
    - Does it include a DA or MDA?
    - What limitations (e.g., temperature) apply if using a WAAS receiver?
    - Can you use a remote altimeter setting with a WAAS receiver?
- What is LNAV+V?
    - At what point does the vertical glide path intercept the MDA?
- What is LNAV?
    - How do you know if you can fly to LNAV minimums?
    - Does it include a DA or MDA?

Another area to cover is the use of visual descent points (VDPs), which are described in AIM 5-4-5. For example:

- What is a VDP?
    - How is the VDP identified on the chart?
    - What techniques are required to fly a procedure with a VDP?
    - If the approach includes a VDP, when may you descend below MDA?

## Missed Approach Procedures

### Missed Approach (AIM 5-4-21 and AIM 5-5-5)

The missed approach procedure (MAP) is one of the most challenging maneuvers a pilot can face, especially when operating alone (single pilot) in IMC. Safely executing the MAP requires a precise and dis-ciplined transition that involves not only aeronautical knowledge and skill—the natural areas of focus in most training programs—but also a crucial psychological shift. There is little room for error on instrument missed approach procedures, and a pilot who hesitates due to deficits in procedural knowledge, aircraft control, or mindset can quickly come to grief. Important MAP topics to cover in the IPC ground review include:

- At what point must you execute the MAP:
  - When flying a precision approach?
  - When flying a non-precision approach?
- What is the proper procedure if the decision to miss is made prior to reaching the MAP?
- Do rules and procedures require you to fly to the filed alternate after a missed approach at the intended destination?
- After executing the missed approach, what factors should you consider when deciding whether to make a second attempt, as opposed to proceeding to an alternate?

## Step 3: Flight Activities

A proficient instrument pilot must possess knowledge and skill in three distinct, but interrelated, areas:

- *Aircraft control skills* (i.e., basic attitude instrument flying, or (BAI)—crosscheck (including effective scan), interpret, and control. If the pilot flies in "glass cockpit" aircraft, the discussion should include appropriate and effective scanning techniques for these aircraft.
- *Aircraft systems knowledge* (i.e., knowledge and proficiency in instrument procedures and aircraft systems, including GPS/FMS, autopilot, datalink);
- *Aeronautical decision-making (ADM) skills* (i.e., higher-order thinking skills, flight planning and flight management, cockpit organization, weather analysis/anticipation).

There may be a temptation to focus the flight portion of the IPC on the first of these three areas (aircraft control), and to proceed sequentially through the required items chart in the PTS (FAA-S-8081-4D). While these activities can provide a snapshot of the pilot's aircraft control skills, a series of approaches and other maneuvers conducted "out of context" will tell you little about the pilot's knowledge of avionics and other aircraft systems, and even less about the pilot's ability to make safe and appropriate decisions in real-world instrument flying.

Having the pilot fly the cross-country trip you assigned and discussed in the ground review is a good way to make a more thorough and integrated assessment of the pilot's knowledge, skills, and judgment. Since ATC procedures are a critical part of instrument flying, ask the pilot to file and fly one leg "in the system." A leg that involves flying from departure to destination gives you an opportunity to evaluate the pilot's communication skills, systems knowledge and day-to-day decision-making skills, including risk management.

The other leg (which can come first, depending on how you choose to organize the exercise) can focus more on basic attitude instrument (BAI) flying, approaches, and holding patterns. For example, you might fly the return leg of the cross-country under VFR, putting the pilot under the hood for BAI exercises. At some point, give the pilot a scenario that requires a diversion (e.g., mechanical problem, unexpected weather below minimums). Ask the pilot to choose an alternate destination and, using all available and appropriate resources (e.g, chart, basic rules of thumb, "nearest" and "direct to" functions on the GPS) to calculate the approximate course, heading, distance, time, and fuel required to reach the new destination. Proceed to that point and, if feasible, do some of the basic aircraft control work (approaches, including circling approach, missed approach, and holding) at the unexpected alternate.

The diversion exercise has several benefits. First, it generates "teachable moments," which refers to those times when the learner is most aware of the need for certain information or skills, and therefore most receptive to learning what you want to teach. Diverting to an airport surrounded by high terrain, for example, provides a "teachable moment" on the importance of obstacle awareness and terrain avoidance planning. Second, the diversion exercise quickly and efficiently reveals the pilot's level of skill in each of the three areas:

- *Aircraft control skills:* The PTS task chart requires one precision approach and one non-precision approach, plus loss of primary flight instruments. Does the pilot maintain control of the aircraft when faced with a major distraction, and/or when flying the missed approach procedure? Consider as well asking the pilot to remove the hood and land out of a practice approach to DA or MDA. For a satisfactory IPC, the pilot should be able to perform all maneuvers in accordance with the Practical Test Standards (PTS) for the pilot certificate that he or she holds. If the pilot is flying a multi-engine aircraft for the check, a single-engine approach is essential.

- *Aircraft systems knowledge:* Does the pilot demonstrate knowledge and proficiency in using avionics and aircraft systems, including GPS moving map navigators and the autopilot? The pilot should be thoroughly familiar with both normal and abnormal operation of all systems, and understand how they work together in IFR flying. In technically advanced aircraft, does the pilot understand the significance of indicators for "ENR," "TERM," and "APR?" Does the pilot correctly manage the sequence for selecting navigation source and arming the autopilot's approach mode? Does the pilot effectively access and manage the information available in onboard databases?

- *Aeronautical decision-making (ADM) skills:* Give the pilot multiple opportunities to make decisions. Asking questions about those decisions is an excellent way to get the information you need to evaluate ADM skills, including risk management. For example, ask the pilot to explain why the alternate airport selected for the diversion exercise is a safe and appropriate choice. What are the possible hazards, and what can the pilot do to mitigate them? Be alert to the pilot's information and automation management skills as well. For example, does the pilot perform regular "common sense" cross-checks of what the GPS and/or the autopilot are doing? Does the pilot always keep track of position when being vectored, using cross radials? Does the pilot maintain awareness of weather, personal minimums and alternates at all times?

# Step 4: Post Flight Debriefing

Most instructors have experienced the traditional model of training, in which the teacher does all the talking and hands out "grades" with little or no student input. There is a place for this kind of debriefing; however, a collaborative critique is a more effective way to determine that the pilot has not only aircraft control skills and systems knowledge, but also the situational awareness and judgment needed for sound aeronautical decision-making. Here is one way to structure a collaborative post flight critique:

    ***Replay:*** Rather than starting the IPC post flight briefing with a laundry list of areas for improvement, ask the pilot to verbally *replay* the flight for you. Listen for areas where your perceptions are different, and explore why they don't match. This approach gives the pilot a chance to validate his or her own perceptions, and it gives you critical insight into his or her judgment abilities.

*Reconstruct:* The reconstruct stage encourages the pilot to learn by identifying the "would'a could'a should'a" elements of the flight—that is, the key things that he or she *would have*, *could have*, or *should have* done differently.

*Reflect:* Insights come from investing perceptions and experiences with meaning, which in turn requires reflection on these events. For example:

• What was the most important thing you learned today?
• What part of the session was easiest for you? What part was hardest?
• Did anything make you uncomfortable? If so, when did it occur?
• How would you assess your performance and your decisions?
• Did you perform in accordance with the Practical Test Standards?

*Redirect:* The final step is to help the pilot relate lessons learned in this flight to other experiences, and consider how they might help in future flights. Questions:

• How does this experience relate to previous flights?
• What might you do to mitigate a similar risk in a future flight?
• Which aspects of this experience might apply to future flights, and how?
• What personal minimums should you establish, and what additional proficiency flying and training might be useful?

# Step 5: Instrument Practice Plan

Offer the pilot an opportunity to develop a personalized IFR skill maintenance and improvement plan. Such a plan should include consideration of the following elements:

*Personal Minimums Checklist:* As noted earlier, one of the most important concepts to convey in the flight review is that safe pilots understand the difference between what is "legal" in terms of the regulations, and what is "smart" or "safe" in terms of pilot experience and proficiency. For this reason, assistance in completing a personal minimums checklist tailored to the pilot's individual circumstances is perhaps the single most important "takeaway" item you can offer. The Personal Minimums Development Worksheet in Appendix 3 is one tool you can use to help the pilot work through issues that should be considered in establishing "hard" personal minimums, as well as in preflight and inflight decision-making.

*Instrument Proficiency Practice Plan:* Many pilots would appreciate your help in developing a plan for maintaining and improving basic instrument flying skills.

*Training Plan:* Discuss and schedule any additional training the pilot may need to achieve individual flying goals. For example, the pilot's goal might be to develop the competence and confidence needed to fly IFR at night, or to lower personal minimums in one or more areas. Use the form in Appendix 7[*] to document the pilot's aeronautical goals and develop a specific training plan to help him or her achieve them.

The IPC is a vital link in the general aviation safety chain. As a person authorized to conduct this review, you play a critical role in ensuring that it is a meaningful and effective tool for maintaining and enhancing GA safety.

---

[*]   of the FAA full version—see online source reference given on Page A3-1.

# References

## 14 CFR §61.57(d)— *Instrument proficiency check.*

Except as provided in paragraph (e) of this section, a person who does not meet the instrument experience requirements of paragraph (c) of this section within the prescribed time, or within 6 calendar months after the prescribed time, may not serve as pilot in command under IFR or in weather conditions less than the minimums prescribed for VFR until that person passes an instrument proficiency check consisting of a representative number of tasks required by the instrument rating practical test.

(1) The instrument proficiency check must be—
- (i)  In an aircraft that is appropriate to the aircraft category;
- (ii)  For other than a glider, in a flight simulator or flight training device that is representative of the aircraft category; or
- (iii) For a glider, in a single-engine airplane or a glider.

(2) The instrument proficiency check must be given by—
- (i)  An examiner;
- (ii)  A person authorized by the U.S. Armed Forces to conduct instrument flight tests, provided the person being tested is a member of the U.S. Armed Forces;
- (iii) A company check pilot who is authorized to conduct instrument flight tests under part 121, 125, or 135 of this chapter or subpart K of part 91 of this chapter, and provided that both the check pilot and the pilot being tested are employees of that operator or fractional ownership program manager, as applicable;
- (iv) An authorized instructor; or
- (v)  A person approved by the Administrator to conduct instrument practical tests.

## AC 61-65E

Completion of an instrument proficiency check: §61.57(d)
I certify that (First name, MI, Last name), (pilot certificate), (certificate number), has satisfactorily completed the instrument proficiency check of §61.57(d) in a (list make and model of aircraft) on (date).

S/S      [date]      J. J. Jones      987654321CFI      Exp. 12-31-05

NOTE: No logbook entry reflecting unsatisfactory performance on an instrument proficiency check is required.

For aviation safety information and online resources, visit www.faasafety.gov

# Checklist for Instrument Proficiency Check

## Step 1: Preparation

- Expectations
- Regulatory Review
- Cross-Country Flight Plan Assignment

## Step 2: Ground Review

- Preflight
- Taxi, Takeoff, Departure
- En route
- Arrival and Approach
- En Route
- Missed Approach

## Step 3: Flight Activities

- Aircraft Control (BAI)
- Systems and Procedures
- Aeronautical Decision-Making

## Step 4: Postflight Discussion

- Replay, Reflect, Reconstruct, Redirect
- Questions

## Step 5: Instrument Practice Plan

- Personal Minimums Checklist
- Instrument Proficiency Practice Plan
- Training Plan (if desired)

# Ground Review

| Pilot | |
|---|---|
| 61.57 | Recency of Experience |
| 91.3 | PIC responsibilities and authority |
| 91.103 | Preflight actions |
| AIM 8 | Medical facts for pilots |

| Aircraft | |
|---|---|
| 91.167 | Fuel requirements |
| 91.171 | Equipment check (VOR) |
| 91.185 | IFR two-way radio communications failure |
| 91.187 | Malfunction reports |
| 91.205 | Required instruments and equipment |
| 91.207 | ELT |
| 91.209 | Aircraft lights |
| 91.213 | Inoperative instruments and equipment |
| 91.411 | Altimeter and pitot-static system tests |
| 91.413 | ATC transponder tests |

| Environment | |
|---|---|
| 91.123 | ATC instructions |
| 91.169 | IFR flight plan |
| 91.173 | ATC clearance and flight plan |
| 91.175 | TO and LDG in IFR |
| 91.177 | Minimum IFR altitudes |
| 91.179 | IFR cruising altitudes |
| 91.181 | Course to be flown |
| 91.183 | IFR two-way communications |
| AIM 1 | Navigation aids |
| AIM 4 | Air traffic control |
| AIM 5 | Air traffic procedures |

| External Pressures | |
|---|---|
| 91.185 | IFR two-way radio communications failure |
| AIM 6 | Emergency procedures |
| AIM 5-6 | National security and interception procedures |

# Flight Activities

| Area of Operation | Date |
|---|---|
| **I. Preflight Preparation** | |
| A. Weather Information | |
| B. Cross-Country Flight Planning | |
| **II. Preflight Procedures** | |
| A. Aircraft Systems Related to IFR Operations | |
| B. Aircraft Flight Instruments and Navigation Equipment | |
| C. Instrument Cockpit Check | |
| **III. Air Traffic Control Clearances and Procedures** | |
| A. Air Traffic Control Clearances | |
| B. Compliance with Departure, En Route, and Arrival Procedures and Clearances | |
| C. Holding Procedures | |
| **IV. Flight by Reference to Instruments** | |
| A. Basic Instrument Flight Maneuvers | |
| B. Recovery from Unusual Flight Attitudes | |
| **V. Navigation Systems** | |
| A. Intercepting/Tracking Navigational Systems and DME Arcs | |
| **VI. Instrument Approach Procedures** | |
| A. Nonprecision Approach (NPA) | |
| B. Precision Approach (PA) | |
| C. Missed Approach | |
| D. Circling Approach | |
| E. Landing from a Straight-in or Circling Approach | |
| **VII. Emergency Operations** | |
| A. Loss of Communications | |
| B. One Engine Inoperative During Straight-and-Level Flight and Turns (Multiengine Airplane) | |
| C. One Engine Inoperative — Instrument Approach (Multiengine Airplane) | |
| D. Loss of Primary Flight Instrument Indicators | |
| **VIII. Postflight Procedures** | |
| A. Checking Instruments and Equipment | |

*Note: Structure the flight portion as an out-and-back IFR XC, with one leg focused on XC procedures (including missed approach and diversion procedures) and the other leg focused on airwork (aircraft control).*

# Pilot's Instrument Experience Summary

Pilot's Name: _____ CFI: _____

Address: _____

Phone(s): _____ e-mail: _____

## Type of Pilot Certificate(s):
☐ Private      ☐ Commercial      ☐ ATP      ☐ Flight Instructor

## Rating(s):
☐ Instrument      ☐ Multi-engine

## Experience (Pilot):
Total time _____ Last 6 months _____ Avg hours/month _____

Time logged since last IPC _____

## Experience (Aircraft):
Aircraft type(s) you fly _____

_____

Aircraft used most often _____

*For this aircraft:*

Total time _____ Last 6 months _____ Avg hours/month _____

## Experience (Flight environment):
*Approximately how many hours have you logged in:*

Day VFR _____ Day IFR _____ IMC _____

Night VFR _____ Night IFR _____ Approaches _____

Approaches to minimums _____ Approaches in last 6 months _____

## Type of Flying (External factors):
*What percentage of your flying is for:*

Pleasure _____ Business _____ Local _____ XC _____

## Personal Skills Assessment:
What are your strengths as a pilot? _____

What do you most want to practice/improve? _____

What are your aviation goals? _____